Copyright 2021 by Legacy Publishing Co.

ALL RIGHTS RESERVED. This book contains material protected under International and Federal Copyright Laws and Treaties. Any unauthorized reprint or use of this material is prohibited. No part of this book may be reproduced or transmitted in any form or by any means, electronic or mechanical, including photocopying, recording, and/or by any information storage and retrieval system without express written permission from the Author/Publisher.

Regarding reliability, accuracy, timeliness, usefulness, adequacy, completeness, and/or suitability of information provided in this book, Eric Skeldon, Legacy Publishing Co., its partners associates, affiliates, consultants, and/or presenters make no warranties, guarantees, representations, or claims of any kind. You agree that Eric Skeldon and/or Legacy Publishing Co. is not responsible for the success or failure of your personal, business, health or financial decisions relating to any company products/services.

No representation in any part of this information are guarantees or promises of any kind. The Authors and Publisher (Eric Skeldon, Legacy Publishing Co. or any representatives) shall in no way, under any circumstances, be held liable to any party (or damages arising directly or indirectly) from any use of books, materials and/or seminar trainings, which are provided "as is" and without warranties.

NIV / NIVUK - Unless otherwise noted, all Scripture references are taken from the NEW INTERNATIONAL VERSION. Copyright ©1973, 1978, 1984 International Bible Society. Used by permission of Zondervan Bible Publishers.

KJV - Scripture quotations from The Authorized (King James) Version. Rights in the Authorized Version in the United Kingdom are vested in the Crown. Reproduced by permission of the Crown's patentee, Cambridge University Press

ESV - Scripture quotations are from the ESV® Bible (The Holy Bible, English Standard Version®), Copyright © 2001 by Crossway, a publishing ministry of Good News Publishers. Used by permission. All rights reserved.

NKJV - Scripture taken from the New King James Version®. Copyright © 1982 by Thomas Nelson. Used by permission. All rights reserved.

NASB - Scripture quotations taken from the (NASB®) New American Standard Bible®, Copyright © 1960, 1971, 1977, 1995, 2020 by The Lockman Foundation. Used by permission. All rights reserved. www.lockman.org

TPT - Scripture quotations marked TPT are from The Passion Translation®. Copyright © 2017, 2018, 2020 by Passion & Fire Ministries, Inc. Used by permission. All rights reserved. ThePassionTranslation.com.

AMP - Scripture quotations taken from the Amplified® Bible Classic,

Copyright © 1954, 1958, 1962, 1964, 1965, 1987 by The Lockman Foundation

THE KINGDOM MIND

By Eric Skeldon, Julia McCoy, Aaron Janda,
and 10 other Kingdom Influencers

Legacy Publishing Co.

∼

"For if you remain silent at this time, relief and deliverance for the Jews will arise from another place, but you and your father's family will perish. And who knows but that you have come to your royal position for such a time as this?"

—Esther 4:14 NIV

∼

What People Are Saying about *The Kingdom Mind*

Now here's a book that will speak Kingdom reality to you! Eric Skeldon, collaborating with other Kingdom Influencers, has given us a treasure! *The Kingdom Mind* will take you into the powerful testimonies of some of God's mighty Kingdom-pullers! They pull the Kingdom of God into the earth by their ministries. I know you will love this book, and may God give us all a KINGDOM MIND! A new Kingdom mind-set will be yours after reading this! Get a copy for a friend—they will thank you for it!

Dr. Brian Simmons

Head Translator of *The Passion Translation*

For those who are looking for authenticity and for those who are seeking a fresh infusion of Holy Spirit power and an understanding of the Kingdom of God, *The Kingdom Mind* will be an inspiration to them on their journey. The raw realities of living life, even a religiously motivated life, without a Kingdom mind-set will be challenged—in a good way. The powerful testimonies shared in this book bring both glory and honor to God. He alone reveals the heavenly mandate for each person to walk in the Spirit, modeling the Kingdom, which doesn't merely come with the enticing words of man's wisdom, but in demonstration and power. *The Kingdom Mind* is a fresh reminder for all to return to a dynamic foundational Kingdom lifestyle.

Dr. Gary Adams

President of Mission Harvest America

The Kingdom Mind is a tapestry of stories about God, His people, and their journeys into His calling. Woven into each story is Romans 8:28, a wonderful biblical promise for believers to answer the Kingdom's invitation to come into our full destinies. It's a collaboration of stories of deliverance, transformation, and restoration. Thank you, Eric Skeldon, for your part in making this amazing book possible.

Gerald Duran

Founder of CanaGlobal

Testimonies are powerful, and this book includes powerful testimonies from present-day Kingdom builders. Are you in need of an encouraging word? Are you looking for more out of your life? This book will leave you saying, "If He can do it for these people, He can do it for me." Be encouraged as you read these uplifting stories and find out for yourself how to live with a Kingdom mind-set.

Joe Winger

Author, poet, and minister of fun

The Kingdom Mind tells the stories of people broken by life and broken by religion, who found healing and freedom through connecting with Jesus. In each chapter, you will find worldly experiences that lure into false fulfillment juxtaposed with beautiful expressions of true intimacy, belonging, and purpose that can only be found when we turn our minds to the Kingdom of God. No matter where you are in your walk with God, you will find inspiration and hope in these pages that will stir in you a longing for a closer relationship with the King of kings. And as you seek Him, you will renew your mind to a clearer view of your true Kingdom identity, so you can step boldly and powerfully into all the blessings that await you.

Dr. Darlene A. Mayo

Neurosurgeon and Neuroscientist, Author of *The Science of God's Healing Power*, Founder of Healing in the Kingdom

This book will help shift your mind-set from a carnal mind-set to a Kingdom mind-set. We hear a lot about "His" Kingdom. Eric Skeldon narrates his powerful story of his journey and redemption. All the principles of God and the sheer presence of God will jump out of these pages as you read this book.This is a very authentic and yet simple story of a man who was born in Alabama and raised the Bible belt of Texas, who joined the military when he was twenty-one years old, and who, once he finished his duty to the country, joined the corporate world of sales and marketing. Eric has many accomplishments under his belt as an entrepreneur, a social media expert, and a YouTuber. He has such an effervescent personality that is hard to not notice him. I highly recommend this book and appreciate all that Eric is doing for the community at large.

Ash Samuel

Owner of Cross Net, Inc.

DEDICATION
BY ERIC SKELDON

I want to honor a mentor of mine, Myles Munroe, whose mandate and mission impacted millions. A great part of my reintroduction to the Kingdom came through his books, teachings, and audio sermons I found online and which I spent hundreds of hours listening to and learning from.

To my beloved wife, Felicia Jewell Skeldon, you spark in me the desire to be a better husband, man, and leader. You shine forth the love of Jesus and help people see who they really are.

To my oldest daughter, Ziona Jewell Skeldon, you are a gift to me from heaven who is full of goodness and grace. To my precious daughter Emerald Rose Skeldon, God has great plans for you. You have a great treasure inside you—do not ever forget it! To my beloved daughter Sapphire Royal Skeldon, you show sophistication and grace. Your prayers as a child demonstrate the love that God has for a hurting world. Esther Reign Skeldon, you were born for such a time as this. To my youngest, Heavenly Glory Skeldon, my youngest daughter of Heaven. You show the glory and majesty and goodness of God. It's a joy to see you always smiling and happy. One of the most peaceful babies I've ever encountered! You will do mighty things on the earth!

As I write this love letter, it is currently April 14, 2021, and I feel the Spirit strong on this:

To the millions of people all over the world who are struggling with identity and purpose, I declare that the stories from this book will illustrate God's love for His people on this planet. I dedicate this book to awakening your dreams and letting you discover your gifts. Do not be afraid of being great for God. God has a plan, a purpose, and a destiny for your life!

FOREWORD
BY JESSE SHAMP

Eric and Felicia Skeldon are a powerful couple whose hearts are to see God's Kingdom advance in the earth. God has mandated them to raise up a generation of Kingdom entrepreneurs. They both carry something that is greatly needed for the body of Christ in this hour. The two of them impart a mind-set of the Kingdom of heaven to the Church that is both impactful and revelatory. I have witnessed this firsthand. The Kingdom mind is breaking the mold of past mind-sets in the Church and is pioneering a new way of conducting ministry in the marketplace.

God is raising up a Kingdom company of entrepreneurs to help fund the end-time harvest in this hour. They are the laborers who have gone out into the field; they are those who will co-labor with ministries to bring in the harvest. The transformation of the mind is the key to unlocking what we have been given access to by our heavenly Father. Old mind-sets and old wineskins have held the Church back from the fruitfulness that God has wanted to produce in His people. There is a generation that will shake the earth with the power and glory of God, the revelation of the Kingdom of God—the "lightnings of God" in the earth. The Kingdom is much more than a message—it is a way of life. Jesus came that we might have abundant life. Creating wealth comes from a Kingdom revelation. As we grasp the revelation that we are sons and daughters of Eden, champions arise. *The Kingdom Mind* carries the keys to unlock groundbreaking revelation for the end-time harvest. Get ready —this book will change your life!

"But thou shalt remember the Lord thy God; for it is he that giveth thee power to get wealth, that he may establish his covenant which he sware unto thy fathers, as it is this day."

—Deuteronomy 8:18 kjv

Jesse Shamp
Founder of Spirit Word Ministries International
Spiritwordministries.org

THE KINGDOM MIND
INTRODUCTION

This book started in my house in Weatherford, Texas, back in 2009. I was a freshman in college, and while I wasn't that great at school, I was an extremely deep thinker. At this time, I had a scholarship in cheerleading and was surrounded daily by my college teammates and peers. Like a madman, I researched everything about the mind and how it worked.

While everyone else partied, I would be at home in my room trying to understand how the brain functioned and how human psychology worked. I came to find just how powerful the mind is. At the age of eighteen, I knew something was wrong because I saw people living such meager lives. Everyone wanted to be cool, craved attention, or were trying to fit in with different cliques. I could not stop thinking about it and wrote a manuscript I entitled *The Power of the Mind*. I printed it off and gave it to my two college coaches, and they were pretty impressed. I also gave it to my roommates and some of my professors. It was good, but I was missing something. I was so young, trying to figure everything out, and I felt like I had discovered something that was beyond me. I guess I had, but I did not discover much of this knowledge until later in my life, while reading books of the Bible like Proverbs and Psalms, which spoke of the struggles of humanity and sin.

Over ten years later, in 2020, I felt God was talking to me about the transformation through which He had taken me. I bought the domain thekingdommind.com since it was available, and then I waited another year. I began speaking on more stages talking about the Kingdom and the mind while sharing stories. This book was birthed out of those stories. A friend of mine named Aaron Janda, who owns Legacy Publishing, eventually approached me, and we talked about this book that I'd had on hold for such a long time.

Here we are now because of the power of testimonies and stories. Don't let your stories and dreams sit on the shelf to die. This book's purpose is to show you that God has a plan and purpose for your life. Everything that you have overcome can help someone else who is dealing with the same situation. Dust yourself off and prepare for an adventure! At the end you will feel empowered to run the race God has called for you to run.

The Kingdom is always connecting, growing, inviting, and ever expanding!

-Eric Skeldon

1

OVERCOMING THE CARNAL MIND

BY ERIC SKELDON

> "Do not be conformed to this world, but be transformed by the renewal of your mind, that by testing you may discern what is the will of God, what is good and acceptable and perfect."
>
> —Romans 12:2 ESV

I was standing on the side of the highway with three state troopers as my life flashed before my mind's eye. There was a pound of high-quality marijuana in the trunk. These troopers were dead-set in their belief that it was mine, and they tried to get permission to search the trunk of the car that belonged to the girl who was my driver at the time. All the memories and decisions that had led up to this moment were burning in my mind. I was thinking to myself, *Man, I messed up, and there is no way out of this.*

So I did what any good child with a praying mom and grandma would do: I prayed and cried out to God. With sweaty hands, I flipped a quarter up and down and anxiously prayed, *God, if You can hear me right now and will rescue me from this, I will know that Jesus is real, and I will follow You the rest of the days of my life.* God heard my prayer that day, and I realized He had always been there, even when I couldn't see it or understand His silence.

Albert Einstein once said, "There are two ways to live your life. One is as though nothing is a miracle. The other is as though everything is a miracle." What happened next still shows me there were angels and the covering of the hand of God over my life since my childhood. After about an hour of fearfully waiting, I was called back over by the three state troopers. One of them said, "Son, today is your lucky day. All the drug dogs are sick. Go home." I could not believe my ears! God had heard me! He came through for me in my darkest hour. I had been running so far from Him, and I didn't even know if He cared, when all along He had been pursuing me. The whole trajectory of my life changed when God intervened on that day.

Let's travel back through time just a bit. I was born in Montgomery, Alabama, and grew up in the great Bible belt of Texas. My parents moved to Atlanta, Georgia, for five years, and while they were there, we attended a Pentecostal church. I remember being a bold prayer warrior as a kid. I would pray for all the evil people and the homeless. I always had a heart for the people who were hurting the most.

I was five when we moved to Lewisville, Texas, in 1996. I spent most of my life in one house, a relatively stable home. My dad, Jeffrey Skeldon, had come to America in the 1980s from Johannesburg, South Africa. My mom, Veronica Solis, grew up in Wichita, Kansas, the youngest of twelve siblings. She is a beautiful Spanish woman with such an awesome appetite for life and adventure. I remember my mom dragging my two brothers and me to church on what felt like every day that ended with a *y*. However, even with a good church upbringing, in Texas we attended big schools, and I wanted to be cool.

The tug-of-war between hanging out with the church-type kids and the "cool" kids at school was a major challenge for me. I wore baggy jeans with NBA jerseys and played basketball almost every day. My dream was to practice and become like a pro, eventually going to the NBA. I did end up being the tallest out of all my brothers, but even being five feet eleven—six feet tall with shoes on—it was still hard to compete in Texas against 5A schools that seemed to have the top basketball players in the country. The competition was tough at Lewisville High School, and while I was trying to be the best in sports, I struggled with my grades and was failing math. I knew I had barely made the junior varsity team, and I would not get any playing time because I was failing. It didn't look good for me in basketball.

Then I heard about our cheer team and how easy it was to get a scholarship for cheer. I started in my junior summer and my senior year of high school and would typically train twice a day. I became good very quickly and saw the potential of what my body and mind was physically capable of doing. I was able to do a standing full and a double full in record time for someone just starting out. If you type into YouTube, *Eric Skeldon Cheer*, you can see the tumbling and stunts I performed.

One thing I disliked about the traditional school system is that it seemed too conventional. I had an exceedingly difficult time with math problems that involved letters with long equations because my brain would switch something up and that would mess up the end answer. This led to low grades and the teachers thinking I was "slow." Some concepts in math did not make sense to my mind, and I needed a lot of extra help, which led to me believing that I was stupid. I also had a stuttering problem, which caused me to have a lot of fear when speaking. It felt like the system had put limitations on me, and I just wanted to give up.

Did you know that Albert Einstein was thought to be retarded by his parents and society because he did not start to speak until the age of four? Einstein went on to invent the theory of relativity and win a Nobel Peace Prize. He was also offered—and declined—the presidency of Israel. The presidency of Israel?! How cool is that? What a wise guy to be offered that opportunity and have the insight to decline. Shortly after the death of Israel's first president, Chaim Weizmann, David Ben-Gurion asked Einstein to become the second president of Israel. Einstein declined, stating that at seventy-three years of age, he was too old for the job and that he lacked the "natural aptitude and the experience to deal properly with people."

What I noticed with God is that He likes taking broken things and expressing His glory through them. He can shine through me when I realize my weaknesses and simply allow Him to step into them. My older brother Grant and I both worked at a big church in Grapevine, Texas, during my junior and senior years of high school. We had Dallas Cowboys players like Tony Romo and his girlfriend at the time, Jessica Simpson, show up, along with Jason Witten. It all seemed so cool to see these successful Christians coming together. Everyone looked like they had it together, with their nice clothes, cars, money, and marriages. Let's just say religion can sometimes seem like a show, but I needed something authentic, real, and raw.

One of my mentors and role models, Myles Munroe, once said, "Young people all over the world are very frustrated. They are very disillusioned. Many of them are turning their backs on religion. They are walking away from the faith of their parents, and most of this is because religion has failed them." This was true for me during my college years, as I found myself spiraling, studying different concepts like metaphysics and psychology, along with how the brain functions. I was off to a good start, with an apartment, a job, and performing well in sports. I still wasn't satisfied.

My roommate at the time mainly partied and smoked weed. I started dealing marijuana in the town where I went to school. Over the next two years, my grades and my focus started slipping. My marijuana business was growing, but my soul was dying. It's interesting how God says in Romans 11:29 that His gifts are irrevocable, because I saw early on that I was gifted in business and entrepreneurship, but I had no leader or guidance to show me how to properly carry it out.

God doesn't take your gifts away even when you use them for your own glory, which later on I saw play out in the lives of people like Beyonce, The Weeknd, and so on. They are such gifted people whom God has blessed, but they don't use their gifts for Him. At that time, I was making more money than I knew what to do with. But I was numb. I figured I was invincible, but really, I was arrogant and naïve. I still thank God and my praying mom that I never got into any real trouble. I was connected one level under the cartel, and even though I told myself I was helping people to gain "medicinal marijuana" and I was researching how the different strains could help the brain, etc., I knew it wasn't what I was supposed to be doing. After being mugged multiple times and losing almost everything, I felt like a gambler or an addict. I would always say, "I just need to get back to where I was, then I can stop dealing drugs." My relationship with God struggled, and that leaked into my relationship with my parents and peers. I was angry all the time. I had so much anxiety and depression. My coping mechanism was to watch porn all the time. I felt like a total failure.

I was running away from God, which led to the lowest point of my life—being in the presence of those state troopers, knowing I was about to go to jail. But God... God showed me He was there for me. When He rescued me from that situation, it woke me up to the fact that He had saved me from my own actions. Had I kept going down that path, I soon would have been killed or locked up for a long time. If I had been busted on that day, I wouldn't have been able to access student loans or get a business degree. I also wouldn't have gotten accepted into the military or gain the training I needed to gain some much-needed discipline. That next week, I was supposed to pick up my first car, one my parents had bought me, and going to jail would have most likely ruined that opportunity as well, along with my reputation. That experience brought me back to God and humbled me.

After that I began to reflect on when I had made that declaration before God rescued me. He kept subtly reminding me of my promise to Him. I ended up slowly but surely cancelling all my contacts and connections to the weed industry. I took a break from school and worked as a server at Olive Garden, then did some photography and film projects on the side. I was broke, and I had nothing, but I was at a starting place to figure out what God wanted me to do with my life. God showed me I should continue to finish what I had started, so I contacted my coach and went back to cheer for my redemption year at WC. After dropping out and failing math twice in college, I was back on campus, focused on school and my team. I learned how to be a leader and became a veteran of the team. We got third place in the nation that year while competing against junior colleges in Daytona Beach, Florida. The winner was Navarro College, which has a series on Netflix and is the best of the best. Funny story: I actually went to try out for the Navarro team in Corsicana, Texas, just to see if I could make it and have a chance to be a champion. I remember I was one of the best stunters, who could still do a standing and running full. I had a great tryout. But when Monica Aldama posted the results, my name wasn't on the list. I remember being angry, knowing I was one of the most talented stumblers there. But when I asked her why I didn't make it, she told me it was because they all knew my previous reputation of being a drug dealer and having a bad attitude. Your attitude determines your latitude. It is true that you could be the best, but if you have a bad attitude, you will not get the opportunity to try. They are a nationally winning team every year, and I'm glad I didn't make it because it caused me to reflect on having a better attitude and changing how I want people to remember me. What was going to be my legacy?

I went on to join the Texas Army National Guard, and then I got married and now my wife and I have four beautiful children... God is funny. He tricked me into going into the army. He brought me into the Airborne Infantry and trained me to be a disciplined warrior. He made me a valuable weapon, and then He enlisted me in God's Army. He trained me how to ambush the enemy; how to lead a team to avoid the traps of the enemy; how to swiftly move without being seen; how to always keep my rifle and weapon with me; how to drop from the sky and take ground and communicate very quickly. Now as a general in God's Army, He has shown me how to repurpose my training to fight in the spiritual realm, how to keep my Bible and the sword of the Spirit sharpened and ready all of my days.

While I was doing drills from month to month in the Guard, God told me, "Finish what you started," and so I enrolled in the University of North Texas. At the time, I had still failed remedial math three times while in community college. Here is an amazing story of how the Kingdom works. Now that I was a member of the Armed Services, when I enrolled in UNT, I sat down with the academic counselor, who let me know that because of my government status, I now was EXEMPT from remedial classes!

I was blown away, starting to see how, if I was following God, He would open up doors I could not open on my own. I chose a new degree called Integrative Studies, which lets you do three majors in one. I chose Business Management, International Studies, and Public Affairs and Community Service. With that path set in place, I only had to pass one major math class. I found two good prior-service army battle buddies to study with, and I passed that math class on my first try. The class was two levels higher than the ones I had previously failed!

From there on, college was smooth sailing, because I was now taking courses about what I liked and enjoyed. Thus, I liked focusing on them, and I didn't get so bored. I recommend, if possible, that you find things you like to do for work. Many times, you will have to do things you do not enjoy, but still, do those things to the best of your ability, as unto the Lord, and your hands will be blessed.

After I finished school, I had more of the confidence of Christ in me. My old mind-set, of being the dumb kid who did not function well in traditional school, had changed to the understanding that "I can do all things through Christ who strengthens me" (see Philippians 4:13). I took that attitude to the marketplace, since I saw that Jesus did 80 percent of His miracles in the marketplace outside of the Church.

I took some courses on professional selling and gained experience selling phones at Sam's Club and garden materials at Home Depot. The great thing about sales is that many times, your pay is determined by your performance. It's also uncapped, which fit my desire and philosophy to not place limitations on my life. I would speak and declare that I would become a multimillion-dollar salesman. It took a year for a sales organization to give me a chance. I still believed and decreed, and a year later, I was given a shot. I landed a software sales position, and I did millions in contract value, but as a business development rep, not the closer.

I went from there to Kansas and found a closing role. I landed a million-dollar client, with around thirty clients total, and I did millions in invoices and hit six figures for the first time in my life.

Death and life are in the power of the tongue (see Proverbs 18:21). If you are ever to do anything great in life, you yourself will have to believe that you can do it. Write it down and declare it until it happens. Don't you dare give up on your dreams, especially when you share the dreams and visions of God that are in your head.

One day in 2019, at a conference in California, I had a deeper revelation of what it means to have the "mind of Christ" (1 Corinthians 2:16 NKJV). It is not me who lives, but "Christ lives in me" (Galatians 2:20 NKJV). God's Kingdom is upside down. It is better to give than to receive (see Acts 20:35).

I started sowing and giving; I would give even when the Holy Spirit would tell me a number that was thousands of dollars, and I really needed the money. You won't learn this in a book or college course about handling money. I had a wife and kids and not the greatest job. Still, I gave what He told me to give and watched as He gave it back to me ten-fold. When I love and serve my wife more and speak kind things even when I don't feel it, I watch as she comes back and loves me even more. No wonder I have five daughters! I watched as I gave God my time, and He gave me more time, multiplying my day. God is not bound to time; He is outside of time. When you give Him the first fruits of your day and your money, just watch what He will do.

When I gave God my mind, He gave me the most brilliant thoughts and ideas from heaven. Remember that heaven is full of solutions. It's the world that is full of problems. When we plug in to the Source, when we gain full access to the mind of Christ, we have the Wi-Fi connection to the "answer book" of the Creator of the universe! Imagine taking the hardest problems society has and accessing the answer key to those problems. Imagine taking the hardest course in college and having the cheat codes given to you from heaven. When we are hooked up, in an intimate relationship with the God who dwells within us, the Kingdom of heaven is within us. Then we can unleash the greatest solutions through the Father's love and restore the broken places, the broken people, the broken world!

We want to see God's glory not only dwell in us, but also dwell in our neighbors and our city, our region, and our world. This is not about us! God lights up our mind and hearts so we become a living river of flowing water. We become beacons of light everywhere we go. That is my mission and what is on my mind for this book—that you will take what you hear and receive from God, then apply this and rise up as an army on fire, who will reign in heavenly glory on the earth for Jesus' sake!

I am a Kingdom entrepreneur in the real estate space taking territory for the Lord. We are expanding our real estate brokerage, looking for agents who haven't attained a license yet to ones who are dominating in sales, selling one hundred houses a year, looking for more time and freedom. Let's lock arms and advance the Kingdom together!

ABOUT ERIC SKELDON

Eric Skeldon is an Innovator, Author, and Speaker who transforms systems and people into their best state. Eric is a Husband and Dad to five princess warriors.

Eric was an Army paratrooper who graduated with a Business Degree from University of North Texas. Later ventured into tech sales and did millions for multiple companies before going to build Kingdom Warriors NFT that is now in 60 nations and impacting thousands through NFT technology and building a Kingdom Media Company that is funding missions.

Eric & Kingdom Warriors Mission is to create a play to earn (P2E) game where you discover identity and learn kingdom principles while earning cryptocurrency and a living wage in Africa.

https://www.instagram.com/realericskeldon

kingdomwarriorsnft.com

2

FROM A CHILD IN A CULT TO A WOMAN WITH A LEGACY: LET YOUR PASSION LEAD THE WAY

BY JULIA MCCOY

"We can change our lives. We can do, have, and be exactly what we wish."

—Tony Robbins

I still remember the hot summers in Pennsylvania, growing up as a little kid in my father's Fundamentalist household. Those summers were laced with two strong memories: the lingering scent in the air of our strawberry and vegetable gardens in full bloom outside, and the pain in my gut right before a beating.

I couldn't ask why. I couldn't ask why I was locked in the basement after a beating that left angry welts on my legs, back, buttocks, and ankles. Most of the time, I didn't even know what had triggered the beating. Did I ask too many questions? Was the look I gave my father not submissive enough? Did I complain in the middle of a grueling afternoon of summer labor, as I painted the rotting walls of the foreclosed-upon fixer-upper church he'd bought? It could have been anything that caused the chain reaction of a horrific beating in the basement, and the words spoken into my ears afterward that cut even deeper than the metal rod he used on my skin.

Leaving in the middle of the night at twenty-one years old was one of the toughest decisions I'd ever made in my life. I know it broke my mom's heart, even though she'd become an abuser, too. I've been disowned for life since leaving. But it was necessary. I could never have started my life, chased my dreams, not to mention gained any sense of self-worth, normalcy, and happiness, if I'd remained trapped in his toxic household.

We had no choice but to do it secretly. My sister and I left after dark, when the house was quiet and asleep, to maintain our safety and health. He'd begun locking us in our room some nights, when I was nineteen and twenty. He claimed it was to "keep us safe"—isn't that the lie the enemy always uses? Deceit using a half-truth, a promise of false security.

Trauma in my life early on drove me to find my passions very early on. At seven years old, I began writing my first book. I escaped through the worlds I created. My first story was filled with Boogeymen and beautiful creatures, a harsh contrast of bad and good, full of imagination and larger-than-life characters. Stories, the written word, and creating my own reality became my favorite way to pass the time. I yearned for it, snuck away to read and write by flashlight. I would make up stories and narrate them to my sister, in classic radio-show style, as we worked on Dad's giant list of home repairs, spending tedious afternoons together trying not to breathe in the fumes of varnish stripper. My sister always begged me to make up another story, tell her one more. And I always did.

Thankfully, the internet was one thing that wasn't taboo in my father's otherwise suppressive house. When I was seven years old, someone donated a computer to my father. I helped Mom learn how to use the internet that year, and I became a master at the different software they had to use for the church before I turned double digits. At twelve, I posted my stories on Writing.com and was told I had an incredible gift. I tinkered around, learning how to make money online. I got my first online paycheck by filling out surveys for cash at thirteen.

But at nineteen, I found myself halfway through college and failing miserably. I'd signed up for a nursing program to try to earn my parents' approval, but it didn't work. Every day, my father found a new reason to express his disappointment in me: My skirt was a millimeter too close to my butt and not loose enough, or my neck was exposed a little too far. Every day, he and my mother came up with new rules that created even more oppression. I couldn't do anything right. It was as if I needed to learn to read his mind. I tried my hardest to rise to the challenge, but reading minds is humanly impossible.

Living in his home was so miserable, I was beginning to contemplate suicide. I Google-searched "how to die painlessly" every other night, thinking a quick death was better than my life. But something in me—I now know it was God and His Spirit, keeping me alive for a greater purpose I had yet to even dream of—nudged me to restart anew on the path of my passion. I did. One morning, at nineteen, I woke up and did another Google search: "how to write for a living." I learned about the world of freelance writing and was enthralled. My eyes lit up when I simply thought about the idea of writing and earning money for my words. I threw myself wholly into learning how to write for a living. Day and night, I began to teach myself how I could make money and establish myself in the online world. I was attracted to creating content that would be found in Google searches (SEO content), since it made sense to me to connect my written words to a clear business growth goal for my clients. I didn't overthink anything—I acted on my intuition. An environment of daily trauma will make your passion so crystal clear, it's as if you can't ignore it. I think it's the unexpected gift God gives abuse victims. Some act on it; some don't. I did. I was up at 4 a.m. every morning, signing up to freelance sites and applying to paying gigs. Three months after I did that first Google search, "how to write for a living," I was earning $1,500 a month—more money than my parents earned in two months—and failing college miserably. (Instead of studying for a boring lab test on pharmaceuticals, I chose instead to answer client calls and write their content for a paycheck. It was a no-brainer to me.)

My passion ultimately led me into the freedom, the success, and the incredible legacy God has given me today—Express Writers, an e-commerce content writing agency, an incredible company with ninety people on staff, and four published books for sale on Amazon. I've created many other side projects and wonderful ventures, too, with my husband and business/life partner, Josh, whom God led me to meet through extraordinary and timely events. I could spend the rest of this chapter on that story, but I've already written a memoir, *Woman Rising: A True Story*, available on Amazon, which you should totally pick up if you're craving more.

Following my passion gave me back my life at nineteen years old, when I was considering death; it gave me an escape route at twenty-one years old (quite literally—I was able to buy a car with cash and then "escape" in that car, taking my older sister with me), and it has brought me incredible success in life, providing me with ninety jobs, earning over $5M in sales through my writing agency, which I'd initially started with nothing more than $75 in the bank. I love every second of what I do.

A big question everyone wants to know when they hear about my history is this: *Why didn't you run from God?* When I left my father's house at twenty-one, I decided in my heart I'd try to find normalcy, and then God. I wasn't sure I'd ever get to know Him.

I had never known Him outside of what was preached to me by my father, a scary, hellfire-and-brimstone version of a mythical creature above the clouds who seemed to drag his followers around on chains. Or so it appeared, in my head. I was scared to death of the God that was preached to me. But what happened when I left my father's house was incredible—*God found me.* My soon-to-be husband, Josh McCoy, brought me to church for the first time, and we began attending a version of church that shocked me, thrilled me, and made me wonder and long for what I saw there. It was a clear, simple, loving God preached about in those churches. No legalistic rules. No this-or-that obligation to be met before becoming a recipient of God's grace. I also saw *real* people in those churches. Genuineness. Authenticity. I began to believe—to hope—that some church leaders weren't one thing in the public eye and quite another behind closed doors with their families. And in the parking lot of one of those churches, with a worship song playing on the radio, God found me. It was a cold fall day in 2012. My heart was overcome with the realization that *He loves me,* unconditionally, and I surrendered my life to Him.

Ever since that day, I can look back and see His hand at every turn of my life. Even looking back to before I truly knew Him, I can see the Spirit, like a Phoenix, watching over me in my father's house. When the beatings were too vicious and I could have suffered brain injuries—when I saw my sister picked up and smashed down against a glass table while shaking, awaiting my turn—when the wind was knocked out of me as a four-year-old, as I was beat up by angry, hard fists and thrown down hard on a hardwood floor—when my parents almost uncovered our plot to leave in the middle of the night—when the neighbors watched us escaping in the night, a phone against their ear—I could have been rerouted by the evil one. *Just one wrong step. Just one.* But there was something more. A higher power. A greater strength. Like a Phoenix rising, dark and shadowless, unseen, but *present*. He was present, in my whole life, and I can see it as clear as daylight today. I am nothing, I was nothing, apart from Him.

Two things were instrumental for me to overcome in my path forward: overcoming a poverty mind-set and embracing my passion in a BIG way.

I was born into a poverty mind-set. My parents made $400 a month as a family of four. Some nights, we didn't have enough to eat. Some winters, we asked for the old coats people were throwing out, so we would have something warm to wear. Those memories are so vivid in my mind, still to this day, that they've made gratitude easy. I am overcome with gratitude for how far God has allowed me to go in life. For how far He has brought me. I don't deserve a second of it. I'm a timid, introverted wallflower if left to myself, yet He's brought me into the limelight in my industry and allowed me to build the skills to back up my reputation. All to Him I owe. I fall to my knees and give Him the glory. A childhood of extreme poverty makes that *so dang easy.*

But here's the money mind-set trap I was in when I left. I was accepting pennies for my talent, not ready to charge more, and afraid to ask for more or change up my habits so I worked less but earned more. I was working hard, not smart—believing it took constant ninety-hour workweeks to produce any amount of a livable wage. I was working my fingers off, earning $15 to $20 per article. Growing up and bred under an abuser, I was missing a key skillset: how to ASK for what I wanted and what I was worth, boldly and unashamedly. I had been bred to be a YES woman. "Yes, dear." "Just do as I say, do what I want, when I want." "Yes, dear." *That* one has been hard to overcome.

The inability to ask for what I was worth I have overcome because of someone who spoke accountability into my life. Very clearly, too: "Julia, you NEED to ask for double that price. Julia, you need to get off manual invoicing and build an e-commerce system to take payments, so life gets easier. Julia, you need to hire an editor. Julia, it's time to hire a manager. Julia, you need to take a break and rest this evening. Will you promise me that you will?" Guess who spoke those words into my life? I am blessed—all of that came from my husband. He has spoken every one of those phrases to me, sometimes multiple times, at different points in my life.

If your husband or partner isn't the one calling you to better standards for yourself (and that's the best option! Your spouse can be your best truth partner), find a friend who will. Ask them to tell you the truths you find hard to tell yourself. This is instrumental so that you stay accountable and get past the growing pains. Today, I boldly ask for what I believe the results are worth to my client. I still fight imposter syndrome; I hear that one never leaves you, and it's a constant work to overcome it. That's okay. I can handle that one. What I can't handle is thinking I'm worth anything less than how God sees me. Yes. God touches the paycheck area, and He gives an abundance mind-set, a spirit of generosity, and the talents we have in our fingers to do good work. *That is all His.* And we are His children. Children don't get the crumbs! They get the main entrée, the delicacies, and the *delights of their hearts.* Psalm 37.4, "Delight yourself also in the LORD, and He shall give you the desires of your heart" (Psalm 37:4 NKJV).

Finally, it's all about embracing your passion in a BIG way. This is where I'll end my chapter in this book. My life is a testimony to this, if you haven't noticed already. I'm just a girl who followed her dream to write for a living, fully and entirely, no holds barred. *You must have no plan B when you're following God's plan A for your life.* And God has given *each one of us a talent.* It's up to us whether we bury it in the earth or use it to multiply what we have by tenfold—to grow our happiness and purpose —because it's incredibly rewarding to walk in your true passion, to grow the lives of others (our clients and students), and to grow the legacy we give to our family.

The question is...*will you?*

Keep going. The best is yet to come!

ABOUT JULIA MCCOY

Julia McCoy is a serial entrepreneur, content marketing strategist, and a passionate advocate of using content to build a business. She teaches courses at The Content Hacker™, leads operations at her writing agency Express Writers, and writes bestselling books.

https://www.instagram.com/fementrepreneur

contenthacker.com

3

AM I LOSING MY MIND?

BY AARON JANDA

"Identity is not what I chose... Identity is what I receive as a result of my relationship with God."
—Pastor Russell Johnson

I feel all alone. Does anyone else feel this way? Alone in my hopes, my dreams, and my desires. It feels like no one understands. I can't be the only one who feels like this, so why isn't anyone talking about it? Who am I, and what is my purpose? These are questions that are so difficult to answer, let alone believe the answers with all the voices screaming in my head!

You know the voices I'm talking about. The ones that tell you that you will never be enough, that you're too lazy, that you don't have the right mind-set, motivation, or capacity to accomplish any of the dreams you have. The voice tells you that your dreams are just crazy, fictional fantasies that you'll never accomplish. Then even more voices scream that no matter how hard you try, you will always fail, because that's who you are—a failure.

Why do I have these thoughts? Why do WE have these thoughts? Could it be because we are on the verge of something incredible? Could it be that we are on the brink of something monumental, something that could change the landscape of the world, the course of humanity? Could it be that not only Satan, but even our own minds and bodies, are afraid of what success will look like? So, in turn, our own minds and bodies do everything they can do to keep us comfortable, to never push us outside of our comfort zone. We feed ourselves the lie that safety is our friend or that the risk is never worth the reward.

I believe that everyone, deep down in the most hidden parts of their souls, know that those lies aren't true. But if we've believed them for so long, how can we correct these issues and imbalances? How do we overcome these thoughts and self-sabotaging beliefs? In a lot of ways, I'm still trying to figure out the answers. Quite possibly, this book could be the answer to some people's questions. Hopefully it is. I've been praying to God to reveal these answers to me. Something tells me that He already has, but maybe I've just been too "busy" and my mind has been clouded with too much noise to hear the answer!

These are words shared with me by a good friend of mine recently. I couldn't have vocalized it any better! How true these statements are. We've discussed these things on numerous occasions and concluded that we cannot control the things that happen to us in life, or the things from our past that may have shaped our negative belief systems. But we *can* control what we do moving forward!

This book is all about having a Kingdom mind-set. But what does that mean? Well, let's break it down. The word *kingdom* is defined as "a domain ruled by a king or a queen." You could be reading this book and not be aware that the Bible describes Jesus Christ as the King of kings and the Lord of lords. Anyone who has been born again and who has a relationship with God has become a part of the Kingdom of God. We will come back to the concept of the Kingdom shortly. But let's talk about mind-set. The word *mind-set* is defined as "a habitual or characteristic mental attitude that determines how you will interpret and respond to situations." Wow! A *habitual* (commonly used) or *characteristic* mental attitude that determines how you will not only interpret what happens in your life but also how you will *respond* to those situations.

Just from a very simple and basic viewpoint, it seems like having a bad mind-set could affect every area of your life in a bad or negative way! It can affect your job, your relationships, your marriage, and your business, just to mention a few aspects of your life. However, on the other side of the coin, developing a good, healthy mind-set can affect all aspects of your life in a good and positive way. I heard an accomplished actor say recently, "You can never bring somebody up if they don't want to go up. You can't, no matter how good you think you are, no matter how much you tell them you can help them. If they don't want to go up, there is nothing you can do." The writers in this book truly want to impart wisdom into your life and help you develop a healthy mind-set, but if you don't want to grow, change, or make the adjustments necessary, there is nothing in the world we can do for you. You have to make the decision on your own. You have to choose what you do from this moment forward. You can't change the past, but you can change your future.

I founded and operate a book publishing company—the same company that is publishing this very book. So, naturally I speak to a lot of writers and people who want to write books. One thing I've realized is that most people don't start to write simply because they don't know where to start. They don't publish their work because they don't know how! So, you may be reading this, and you're saying, "Aaron, I see the value in developing a healthy mind-set, and I want to do that, but I don't know how or even where to start." Now, there are thousands of books out there on changing your mind-set, speaking positive affirmations, and in some cases, tricking your mind into believing certain things. I can't say I recommend all of them, but there are some pretty good ones out there. Remember when I defined the words *kingdom* and *mind-set* earlier? Well, I don't want to help you develop just a positive or a healthy mind-set, I want to propose that there is an even better way—and that is to develop a "Kingdom mind-set"!

In the Bible, Romans 12:2 says, "Don't copy the behavior and customs of this world, but let God transform you into a new person by changing the way you think. Then you will learn to know God's will for you, which is good and pleasing and perfect" (NLT). Another translation (NKJV) says it this way: "And do not be conformed to this world, but be transformed by the renewing of your mind, that you may prove what is that good and acceptable and perfect will of God." You must let God transform you into a new person by changing the way you think. You must be transformed by the renewing of your mind, so that you may be able to prove what is the perfect will of God.

As Christ followers, we are told that not only can we change the way we think, but we can also be transformed by renewing our minds! That's incredible! But what does that really mean? I personally believe that as we read the Bible, the Word of God, the way we think can and will change. I believe that as we read and study God's Word, our minds can be renewed to the point that we can *know* what the perfect will of God is for our lives. We can know His will concerning everything we do—whether in business, in our family lives, in our careers, in every area!

The Bible talks about a man, King Solomon, who was the wisest person to ever live on the earth. There will never be another person who is wiser than he was. He wrote a lot of significant things in the Bible, and I don't know about you, but I want to glean from his wisdom! I also don't think that it's a coincidence that there are thirty-one chapters in the book of Proverbs—written primarily by King Solomon—one for every day of the month! That would be a perfect place to start your reading, especially as you venture out into new business projects and new relationships!

What having a Kingdom mind-set looks like to me is allowing the Bible to transform the way I think to the point that I look at every situation the way God would see it and take action accordingly! The Bible says that there is nothing new under the sun. Did you know that there isn't a single situation that we can encounter in life that the Bible doesn't reference to or share with us advice on how to handle them? We truly do have all the tools we need to experience the life that God has planned for us, but we still have to *choose* to pursue it.

Proverbs 25:2 says, "It is the glory of God to conceal a matter, but the glory of kings is to search out a matter" (NKJV). If you want to live like a king, if you believe what the Bible says, "that we are kings and priests" (Revelation 1:6 NKJV), then you need to start doing the things that kings do: search out wisdom, seek out what God's will is for your life, and pursue your purpose. But you aren't going to be very productive if you are just doing things the same way you have always done them. You have to make a decision to seek out wisdom, to allow the Word of God to transform the way you think and renew your mind! He will give you a Kingdom mind!

ABOUT AARON JANDA

Aaron Janda is originally from Seattle, Washington. He is a two-time Amazon Bestselling Author, Publisher, Speaker, and Serial Entrepreneur. Aaron authored his first book *My $100 Dollar Project,* a book that challenges readers to take $100 and multiply it to $1,000 and beyond. Aaron co- authored his second book, *Influence and Income Online,* which became an Amazon #1 Bestseller in five categories. Aaron co-authored his third book, *Overcoming Adversity In Entrepreneurship* which went on to be an Amazon #1 Bestseller as well!

Aaron has launched multiple six-figure businesses. In the last few years he had lost everything twice and had to rebuild his life and business for a third time. He will be sharing more of his story in his two upcoming books, *Your Story Matters* and *Don't Quit!* Aaron is passionate about helping others and sharing his story in hopes that it may challenge someone who also could be facing seemingly impossible situations or circumstances to not quit or give up! If you would like to book Aaron to speak at your school, organization or event, contact him for more information at the email below.

Aaron is the Founder of Legacy Publishing Co., in Tulsa, Oklahoma. "Changing The World One Reader At A Time."

https://www.instagram.com/aaronjanda

legacypublishingco.com

4

INTIMACY WITH GOD: THE "KNOWING"

BY FELICIA SKELDON

Let me tell you a little bit about myself. My name is Felicia Skeldon, and I am the wife of Eric Skeldon, the man who felt pressed by God to get a whole bunch of Kingdom collaborators into a group to write this book together. As a kid, I went to various church camps and attended church services every now and then. I did not come from a stable home, which was not the best way to grow up. After being abandoned by my biological father when I was just a baby, I was molested by a family member at the age of four and experienced some intense abuse. My life seemed to consist of trauma after trauma, and now that I am older, I can see more clearly how the enemy intended to flood my existence with the same turmoil that he had embedded in the lives of my mother and grandmother. I was introduced to porn when I was eight years old, and the addiction did not end for me until I was eighteen. Jesus didn't become real to me until I was sixteen, when my grandma bought the book *23 Minutes in Hell* for me to read. This book scared me so bad that for almost a month, I stopped partying and doing drugs and dedicated my life to Jesus.

Unfortunately, about a month later, I was tempted to go back to my old ways. I knew I had really messed up, because once I turned back to my old life, new doors were opened, to homosexuality, stronger drugs, and a deeper desire for porn than ever before. There is a verse in the Bible that says, "When an impure spirit comes out of a person, it goes through arid places seeking rest and does not find it. Then it says, 'I will return to the house I left.' When it arrives, it finds the house unoccupied, swept clean and put in order. Then it goes and takes with it seven other spirits more wicked than itself, and they go in and live there" (Matthew 12:43–45 NIV). That became my life for two years. Everything grew worse and more perverse than ever before.

Then, when I was eighteen years old, God found me again, in Dallas, Texas, in the parking lot of a nightclub that was a strip club during the day until 2 a.m. and opened for raves from 4 a.m. to 8 a.m. My friends and I were high on Ecstasy, and as we left the club, a girl stopped our car and knocked on the window. She asked if we had any needs she could pray for. We asked her to pray for us to have a safe trip home. God must have taken that prayer literally, because after she prayed, my entire life was headed straight for heaven! I remember being so high that I couldn't talk to God through just my head, so I grabbed a piece of paper out of the center console of the vehicle and wrote Him a letter. I told Him that I knew I was going to go back to Satan after that night, but I asked Him to please keep pursuing me. I saw that the girl who had approached us was from a church group that was handing out bottles of water and orange juice to people coming out of the club. When she asked if we wanted one, of course I chose the orange juice because it increases your high. (I don't think the girl knew that when she was passing out the bottles.) I knew that I should have picked the water to hydrate myself, and God later revealed to me that I had denied the Living Water in that moment. I turned the trance music back up and tried to get back into my high.

Within two months of that encounter, I lost everything. My boyfriend at the time, who had become my "god," dumped me. I lost my car, I lost my phone, and I was kicked out of my grandma's house after she had taken me in. Everything was gone. The only thing I had left was an offer to live at my mom's place while she was recovering from her meth addiction.

I started attending AA meetings with my mother. I watched as people stood up and talked about how only a higher power could save them from their addiction to drugs and sex. Literally, I felt something lift from my eyes and my head. I heard the word "epiphany" spoken to me, and I immediately Googled where that word comes from and the definition. I had obviously heard that word before, but there was something new about it that I had to discover. This is what Google showed me: The Greek word *epiphaneia* means "appearance" or "manifestation," and it refers to the manifestation of Jesus Christ to the world (*MacMillan Dictionary*). I was stunned. Later, I found out that the term *epiphany* is used to describe an event when the supernatural invades the natural.

This experience began my wild and enticing journey of finding out who this God really was and why He wanted me so badly. I realized that I had been seeking love through all the wrong things. Having orgies or masturbating to porn was never going to fulfill me. Using hallucinogens and tripping on drugs would never open the doors of mystery or revelation for my life. None of those things felt the same anymore. I couldn't go back. I started attending Friday night Bible studies with my mom and church every Sunday. I ended up writing out my testimony and giving it to everyone in school. They had all known me as the crazy party girl, and soon a lot of them joined me at the

Wednesday night youth services. I got to watch one of the girls with whom I had had sexual relations get baptized, along with two of my best friends and my sister. We were all baptized on the same day! I still cry just thinking about it. My life would never, ever be the same.

Little did I know, there was a girl who went to my school and had watched me from afar. At one point, we had been dating the same guy without knowing it. She found out he was cheating before I did, and for whatever reason, she would find herself waking up in the middle of the night to pray for me. Later, she told me she would ask God why He was having her pray for someone with whom her boyfriend had been cheating on her. When she found out I was going to be reading my testimony at my church, she asked if she could come. She cried as I read it and afterward came up to me and told me how sorry she was that she had judged me without knowing everything I had been through. We became best friends and ended up visiting so many churches in our city where God was moving. We ended up attending Bible college together when we moved to Franklin Springs, Georgia. Her mom moved there in faith after being told by a prophet that she would die spiritually if she stayed where she was. She ended up getting a job at the college, which granted free tuition to two of her other daughters as well! We watched as miracle after miracle took place. I knew God was preparing me for something greater, and I studied like crazy. At the age of twenty, though, I ended up having a mental breakdown and took a turn for the worse. A lot of the trauma I experienced had caught up to me. Thankfully, free counseling was offered at the college, and the counselor walked me through my dissociation, healing, and therapy with the Holy Spirit. I realized that I had been trying to perfect my walk with God by fasting, praying, and not sinning to the point that it had turned into a religious addiction. My religious OCD grew so severe that I stopped eating as a "sacrifice for God," and at one point, I went nine days without sleeping. My thoughts would not slow down, and I would obsess over Scripture to the point that my body formed a tic every time I thought I was sinning in my mind. I would jolt my head and quickly repent so that God would save me from my distress. I became convinced that I needed to suffer like Job in order to prove my love for God. This continued for years but got better as I stayed on medication and remained in therapy. By the grace of God, I graduated with an associate's degree and returned back home to Texas.

My discovery of God's love increased as I allowed myself to receive it. There were so many lies for me to get past, but He uncovered them all. The biggest hurdle I had to cross was the understanding that God was my dad, and that I didn't have to earn my role in His family. God is my dad. There is nothing I can do for Him to cause Him to love me less, and there is nothing I can do for Him to cause Him to love me more. He loves me because He loves me, because He loves me, because He loves me, because He loves me, because He loves me, because He loves me, because that is what He is! God is love (see 1 John 4:8). The very essence of love is who He is, and He cannot go against His own nature. The most incredible realization is that we will forever be discovering His love for us because He is infinite. The love He has for us will never cease to exist or amaze. The fact that I am able to write this chapter is a declaration of His love to everyone who reads it. There were times when my panic attacks were so severe that I couldn't pick up a book, let alone the Bible. Writing, calling someone on the phone, having a conversation, or meeting up with someone was nearly impossible because of my anxiety, and it became debilitating once it turned into depression. I am convinced that God has placed doctors and counselors on this earth to help us make sense of the things we endure in our lives. Even Moses himself had to appoint counselors in the Old Testament to help the people of Israel because the work was too much for him (see Exodus 18:18–25 NIV). We must not only count on the pastors who are leading the churches. We need everyone working together in one accord to help heal and deliver those in the body of Christ who are still suffering. If it wasn't for the counselors, therapists, doctors, teachers, pastors, prophets, evangelists, and apostles whom God placed in my life, I wouldn't be here. Many times, suicide seemed like the only option for me. I have lost a best friend and a sister-in-law to the same issue. The only thing I have found to help withstand mental illness and suicidal thoughts is the love and true intimacy of God.

An intimate relationship with God is nothing short of mystical. Our entire existence consists of one thing: discovering our present oneness with the Creator through His Son, Jesus Christ. The sole purpose of the Gospel is to bring humanity back to the Garden. Throughout Scripture, we find words that are absolutely mind-blowing once we discover their root word and true meaning. I believe that God desires for us to do it this way so that He may usher us into the depths of His wonder. Psalm 42:7 says that "deep calls unto deep" (NIV), while Proverbs 25:2 states that "it is the glory of God to conceal a thing: but the honour of kings is to search out a matter" (KJV). God desires us to search out what the Word is really saying, even when it seems like the words are quite clear. I will go over a few terms that reveal this truth. We will start with the word *mystery*, which occurs twenty-seven times in the King James Bible. This word translated in the *Strong's Concordance* is the Greek term *mysterion*, which literally means "a hidden or secret thing, not obvious to the understanding." There are fourteen Scriptures that are most pertinent:

He answered and said unto them, Because it is given unto you to know the mysteries of the kingdom of heaven, but to them it is not given.

—Matthew 13:11 KJV

Now to Him who has the power to establish you according to my Gospel and the preaching of Jesus Christ, according to the revelation of the mystery which was kept secret since the world began.

—Romans 16:25 KJV

But we speak the wisdom of God in a mystery, even the hidden wisdom, which God ordained before the world unto our glory.

—1 Corinthians 2:7 KJV

Let a man so account of us, as of the ministers of Christ, and stewards of the mysteries of God.

—1 Corinthians 4:1 KJV

For he that speaketh in an unknown tongue speaketh not unto men, but unto God: for no man understandeth him; howbeit in the spirit he speaketh mysteries.

—1 Corinthians 14:2 KJV

Behold, I shew you a mystery; we shall not all sleep, but we shall all be changed.

—1 Corinthians 15:51 KJV

Having made known unto us the mystery of his will, according to his good pleasure which he hath purposed in himself....

—Ephesians 1:9 KJV

How that by revelation he made known unto me the mystery; (as I wrote afore in few words, whereby, when ye read, ye may understand my knowledge in the mystery of Christ).

—Ephesians 3:3–4 KJV

And to make all men see what is the fellowship of the mystery, which from the beginning of the world hath been hid in God, who created all things by Jesus Christ....

—Ephesians 3:9 KJV

This is a great mystery: but I speak concerning Christ and the church.

—Ephesians 5:32 KJV

And for me, that utterance may be given unto me, that I may open my mouth boldly, to make known the mystery of the gospel....

—Ephesians 6:19 KJV

Holding the mystery of the faith in a pure conscience....

—1 Timothy 3:9 KJV

Even the mystery which hath been hid from ages and from generations, but now is made manifest to his saints: To whom

God would make known what is the riches of the glory of this mystery among the Gentiles; which is Christ in you, the hope of glory.

—Colossians 1:26–27 KJV

That their hearts might be comforted, being knit together in love, and unto all riches of the full assurance of understanding, to the acknowledgement of the mystery of God, and of the Father, and of Christ....

—Colossians 2:2 KJV

As seen above, the mystery of Christ is for us to discover. Most of us know that the main goal of Christ was to reconcile you and me back to God without penalty of our sins. We can now ask for forgiveness by coming boldly to the throne of grace to receive His mercy (see Hebrews 4:16 KJV). However, what is not commonly taught in the Church is the oneness that this great gift has bestowed upon us! Right before Jesus was to be crucified, He prayed, "That all of them may be one, Father, just as you are in me and I am in you. May they also be in us so that the world may believe that you have sent me" (John 17:21 NIV). Jesus' main goal was to bring us back into the oneness that Adam and Eve first had with God in the Garden of Eden. This oneness is so intimate that it is greater than any level of intimacy a human being can have with another human here on earth. There is a "knowing" that you and God can have, which can never be diminished. This "knowing" can be found in Genesis 4:1, where it describes the sexual intercourse that took place between Adam and Eve:

And Adam knew Eve his wife; and she conceived (KJV).

The term *knew* in this verse is the Hebrew word *yaw-dah'*, which means "to be known fully." The reason this term is so significant is that the Hebrew language is known to be one of the most poetic languages in the world, especially considering how one word can have many different meanings. The word *know* translated in Hebrew can carry two completely different meanings, depending on how the term is used in a sentence. For example, the "knowing" of a brother would be a different Hebrew term than the "knowing" of a spouse. In the verse above, the type of "knowing" is clearly describing the intimacy that takes place between two lovers. This same term can be found in other verses that God desires us to discover, such as in Jeremiah 1:5: "Before I formed you in [your mother's] womb I knew you" (NASB). When you type this Scripture into *Strong's Concordance*, you will find that the Hebrew word "knew" is the same word, *yaw-dah'*, and it reveals God's true intent all along: oneness. Another spectacular verse is Psalm 46:10: "Be still, and know that I am God" (NKJV). The beauty of this "knowing" is that we can do absolutely nothing to receive it. In Hebrew, the literal translation of "be still" in this verse means to "cease striving." We must cease striving if we ever want to discover how God knows us. He has always known each of us. Our relationship with God was never meant to be based on to-do lists or attending a Bible study or Sunday service at our local church. When we come from a place of awareness of the fact that we are already known by Him, then we will no longer feel that we need to earn His love or affection. It is already there for the taking!

ABOUT FELICIA SKELDON

Felicia Skeldon is the wife of Eric Skeldon and the mother of their 5 daughters, Ziona Jewell, Emerald Rose, Sapphire Royal, Esther Reign and Heavenly Glory Skeldon. She earned a Bible degree from Emmanuel College in Franklin Springs, GA and now resides in Wichita, Kansas. Her profession is studying childlikeness through staying at home with her children and practicing the presence of God moment by moment.

https://www.instagram.com/feliciaskeldon

5

LOCKED UP ABROAD
DAVID SAUCEDA

Day One of Twenty-Three Days Locked Up Abroad. The call that we were waiting for came that our shipping container had arrived from Southern California full of our household goods. After almost ten months of a fruitless job search, we had decided that maybe the doors in California were closed for a reason. My wife and I sat down one evening and brought out our poster board to map out what we envisioned—kind of a vision board or mind map. We sensed that God was at work, and we needed to learn where He needed us to go. We had never been afraid to fulfill our calling as educators, and we also knew that as believers, our jobs and location didn't define us. Our compass was set to "true north," and our mission in life was simple: Follow the King. As the old song says, "Where He leads me, I will follow…"

It was almost three o'clock in the morning, and I began to wonder when David Webb—aka Jason Bourne—would come rushing down the long corridor. Eight hours had passed since I had reported to the port of call to identify some objects found in our shipping container with our household goods.

Mr. Mohammed met me at the entrance of the port of call. When I informed him that my driver was waiting and asked if I should have him leave or wait there, Mr. Mohammed indicated that my driver should leave and not wait. I motioned to the driver to go ahead and leave, telling him I would call him shortly. I expected my visit to the port of call would be over quickly as I had an idea of what the concern might be. We took the elevator to the second floor and walked into a large conference room with metal tables, several computer monitors on a desk in the right-hand corner of the room, and a few seats around another particular table.

"Mr. David, what is the purpose of your being in this country?" Mr. Mohammed sat down and asked. I informed him that both my wife and I were educators and that my wife was working for their government schools. He asked a few more questions about where had we lived before coming to Abu Dhabi, and again, what kind of work I did. Our shipment had arrived two days before, after which it was inspected and released to us by the Port of Abu Dhabi, complete with stamps and the "official" Port of Abu Dhabi tape.

It had been nearly seven months since we had packed up our family belongings in California to be shipped across the world, to Al Reem Island in Abu Dhabi. When the boxes and furniture arrived, it was like Christmas as we opened up box after box and set up our familiar furniture in our luxurious high-rise overlooking the Arabian Sea. Our son Christian immediately noticed that his Air-soft gun and his treasured empty .22 shotgun casings were missing from the shipment. The casings were mementos from Pop-Pop's hunting days, long before he had passed away in Maryland from Parkinson's disease.

Several officers came into the room and placed the Air-soft gun and the empty shotgun casings on the table. "Mr. David, can you identify these items found in your shipment from California?"

Time seemed to drag on as the interrogation by the American equivalent of the CIA in Abu Dhabi continued. My new Nigerian acquaintance assured me that everything would be fine and not to worry about a thing, informing me that he himself had been locked up several times in Dubai, Lagos, and Johannesburg. A stench of fear and sweat emanated from the older Bangladeshi man seated only inches to my left. The odor permeated the small holding area as officers came in and out, apparently joking with the officer seated at the desk in the corner. My Nigerian acquaintance let me know that these men coming in and out were actually plainclothes officers. Most of them were dressed in regular Western wear—jeans, a T-shirt, and a stylish baseball cap. Others, however, came in dressed in the pristine white men's tunic known as a kaftan.

It was nearly four in the morning when I noticed my cell phone ringing on vibrate. It was my wife. After about ten declined calls, I finally asked to go to the restroom. When I was alone, I quietly took out my phone and dialed her number. When she answered, I whispered, "I'm okay. They are questioning me now, so please stop calling."

"Where are you?" she pleaded. I explained that I would soon be released once everything was cleared up. I actually had no idea where I was. I didn't know whether I would be released soon. I didn't have a clue about anything that would happen next, but I wanted to calm my wife and family—at least until I could figure out what else I could do, besides blowing things up and jumping out of the building Jason Bourne–style.

I hadn't yet felt fear or panic at this point. I figured this interrogation was just part of their government's formality to have an

American in the equivalent of our CIA system. My credentials would have to be run through Interpol and other international security agencies to ascertain what level of a threat I presented to their country.

At around five-thirty in the morning, the older Bangladeshi man seated on my left, another Arabic man seated on my right, and I were all instructed to stand up slowly and begin walking forward. This was my first time to walk in shackles. We were escorted down a long corridor, then we entered an elevator to finally exit into the hot, musty desert air. I looked around and tried to take note of where we were. There were a number of tall buildings; some looked like office buildings, but most seemed to be run-down apartments rising eight or ten stories high. Cars had been parked facing the buildings. This wasn't an area of the city that I was used to. It was more run-down, with only a few newer office buildings that had storefront neighborhood markets on the ground floors, dry cleaners, and what looked like a flower shop.

I took my first steps behind the old Bangladeshi man toward a beat-up-looking, older passenger van, and the Arabic man followed behind me by about two feet. The old man struggled to climb up on the little step to enter the vehicle while the officers offered no help. With my hands and feet in shackles, I did my best to push the old man up. He fell on his knees into the passenger van and slowly stood back up. I then carefully lifted each of my feet onto the step and tried not to fall down, considering I was limited to about a foot of chain in front of me and a foot in the back. Once the three of us were situated in the second row seat, the two officers took their places in the front. There was no small talk, no mention of our destination. This was not only my first time in shackles; it was my first time in a passenger van shackled between two other men with metal grates separating us from the drivers in the middle of the night in the Arabian Peninsula.

As the clanky passenger van pulled away from the building where I had been interrogated over the last twelve hours, I tried to determine where I had been taken and where we were headed. I quietly pulled out my cell phone and tried to dim it's light so I could text my wife and ask her to contact our good friends Joey and Amir to get their help. I was seated on the second row and knew it was a huge risk—the officers might confiscate my phone—but it was worth it to at least let my wife know that I was being moved.

After entering a roundabout, the driver made a turn away from the city, toward what seemed like the desert. I immediately realized my situation was not going to improve. I began texting Joey and Amir as well as my wife. They would know how to reach the American Embassy and alert other Americans whom we had become friends with during the previous six months. They would begin to pray. I was exhausted and cold. My mouth was dry and sticky.

The drive took about thirty-five minutes from the center of the city to the outskirts. We drove down a dusty road and approached a gate, which opened to let us in. The building beyond the gate looked newer. Some officers came to open the doors of the passenger van and helped us disembark. We entered the building through a side door from a covered carport area and were escorted into a brightly lit room. The officer inside instructed us to remove all of the contents from our pockets—phone, wallet, watches, and jewelry—and place them in a metal shoebox. We then were told to place the box into a locker, which the same officer locked. We had been transferred to a temporary holding facility and were advised that we would be there until our court hearings. The officer opened a large metal gate, then pointed toward a large bunker room and said, "Find a bed. In the morning you will be taken to the court for your hearing."

In the room, stainless tables had bench seats attached to sit on. The three of us sat down, and an officer asked if we were hungry. The old Bangladeshi man and the Arabic man nodded, and the officer came back with our meals. When I lifted the lid off of a metal cafeteria plate, the food looked like a watered-down version of Mexican *fideo* [a type of angel hair pasta in a very light broth], salad, and a piece of fruit. I declined. I wasn't hungry, and the smell nauseated me. The two other men almost licked the stainless steel plates clean. I motioned for them to go ahead and eat my food as well. I only drank the bottle of water I had been given.

An officer on the other side of the bars watched us through the bars covered with large sheets of Plexiglas. At least six stainless tables were situated in the center area, and on each side wall were what looked like individual cells with one bunk each. The lights were off, and it was clear that men had been locked into those small cells to sleep.

It was increasingly evident that I was not going to go home in the morning, or any time soon, for that matter. I suddenly became nauseated, and the exhaustion of the last eighteen hours hit me like a wall. I knew I had to push on and begin to prepare for life behind bars.

Six Months Earlier: Orange County, California. My wife and I had lived life with the understanding that we were on a journey and we were anchored by our faith in Jesus Christ. Living close to family and lifelong friends in Southern California was special to us. We could drive to be with any of our friends and family in under two hours. We had not even an inkling of desire to leave our beautiful life near the Pacific Ocean, near our loved ones.

However, when you realize doors aren't opening up, you begin to wonder, "Okay, job interviews are happening, and some great connections are beginning to happen, but I still need a paying job." After round-two interviews, significant salary offers were discussed, with more zeroes after the comma than I had ever seen on a paycheck before. But then, after several more weeks, I received two almost simultaneous calls from two different school districts: "Mr. Sauceda, the superintendent and her cabinet were extremely impressed with your second interview. However, the position has been offered to an internal candidate."

We began realizing that the employment doors in Southern California were not going to open up. It was time to consider looking out of state—maybe even out of the country. With openness in our hearts, we asked the Lord, "Where do You want us or need us to be?" We had already determined that God had a mission outside of the country for us, but where?

One night, after we were already in bed, I discovered a website that was seeking qualified school administrators and teachers in Abu Dhabi. Where in the world was Abu Dhabi? Immediately, we looked on Google Maps and discovered a tiny speck of a country in the Middle East. We had many questions and concerns, but we did our due diligence to address them all.

A month later, after having submitted the required application, résumé, and cover letter, we received an email asking us to schedule a phone interview. During the interview, they informed me that they no longer needed male school administrators and thanked me kindly. I quickly interrupted the gentleman on the phone: "Wait, my wife is a fantastic teacher and comes highly regarded!"

He said, "Put her on the phone."

Soon we were packing up our household goods. We asked each of our two kids to identify some items they wanted to put into the shipping container, since the Abu Dhabi Education Council would be paying for our move overseas. It didn't make sense to leave all our things in a rental storage facility for the duration of the two-year contract. Our son had just turned fifteen, and our daughter was going on twelve. Boxes were packed and clearly marked "Christian's Room," "Natalie's Room," "Master Bedroom," "Kitchen," "Family Room," and "Storage." Christian had an affinity for Air-soft guns, as well as his collection of RC cars and off-road vehicles and a few empty shotgun shells that he had as mementos from PopPop's hunting days. Natalie, of course, had lots of books, some collector dolls, and a plethora of Barbie and Polly Pocket dolls.

We boarded the most luxurious airliner we'd ever seen and sank into the business class seats, to be treated like royalty for the twenty-two-hour flight from Los Angeles to Abu Dhabi's beautiful futuristic International Airport. We soon settled into our beautiful high-rise apartment and waited for our shipping container full of our household goods to arrive.

Day Two: Jury, Judge, and Trial. I had finally fallen asleep in a lower bunk of one of the cells that held about ten bunk beds. Before I knew it, the jailer could be heard calling out names. "*Amerique!*" he shouted several times. I didn't realize it was me, the American, whom he was calling. When I opened my eyes, I noticed I was curled into a fetal position and covered with a blanket with my shoes still on. I was in a fog of exhaustion. I could see that at least half of the beds were empty, but I could still hear the harmonious snoring from the upper and lower bunks in my cell. The guard banged the iron gate once more and yelled out, "*Amerique!*"

The shackles on my feet dragged on the ground as seven of us were marched out to load up into a passenger van for our trip to the court hearings. I expected to enter a courtroom such as we have in America. But when we arrived, I was unchained and escorted to a waiting area outside what appeared to be an office. I sat in the black fake-leather club chair to await my arraignment. The Air-soft guns and the empty shell casing were resting on a coffee table as "evidence." One man was seated behind a desk and another had pulled up a chair next to the desk. I was asked to stand in front of the desk and then state my name and the nature of my business in Abu Dhabi.

"My wife and I are educators, sir," I began. "My wife teaches for ADEC [the Abu Dhabi Education Council]."

They looked at the Air-soft gun and empty casing on the coffee table, and then at me. "Mr. David, we must understand why you brought these weapons into the country in your shipping container."

"Sir, the Air-soft gun is a toy. They are sold in this country also. Kids can go play using them at the Al Wahda Mall in Abu Dhabi."

The senior official behind the desk shook his head, then informed me that they must send the casings and Air-soft gun to their weapons and forensics department for an evaluation. I would be released only once all was determined to be okay. "Inshallah, Mr. David, you will be home in a day or two."

I was relieved as I returned to the holding cell, but only a few hours later, I learned I was to be transferred to Al Wathba Maximum Security Prison in the desert. Just before the transfer, a prisoner from Nigeria approached me. In a very prominent Nigerian accent, he said, "Sir, God has a plan." He handed me a small booklet filled with daily devotions from his church, Christ Embassy.

Day Twenty-Three: "*Amérique Farage!*" I could hear people shouting, including several of the guards. After my arraignment, I had been almost immediately transferred to a maximum-security prison for the duration of the "forensic investigation" of the plastic Air-soft gun in our shipping container. I had been deemed an international arms dealer.

As I was being escorted out of my prison cell, my mind quickly raced to my first night in the prison, when I shared with the men in our cell that God always has a purpose and that He redeems all things. I could still hear the voices of almost twenty men singing "Lord, I Lift Your Name on High," echoing from the walls of our tiny cell. As I walked past the window ledge just outside my cell, my mind flashed back to a few nights before, when at two in the morning, I had sat with Daniel from Colombia, and said, "Daniel, I sense you are carrying a huge and unbearable load. Can I ask what it is you are carrying?" Daniel lowered his head into his hands and quietly said in Spanish, "*La pena, estoy cansado.*" He was exhausted from his burden of shame. I responded, "Daniel, I believe that tonight, God wants to set you free. He already paid the price for your sins, and He wants to have a relationship with you."

Daniel lowered his head even further and said, "I don't want my family to be ashamed of the man that I have become. What will my legacy be?"

"Daniel, I said that tonight is the night you can release all the guilt and shame. Is there any reason you cannot surrender your life to Jesus Christ right now?" Daniel said he was ready to surrender.

The next day, Daniel rushed into my cell and said, "David, you are not going to believe what my wife told me when I called home. Two nights ago, my wife's brother, who is a pastor in Colombia, stopped unexpectedly by the house and said to my wife, 'We must pray for Daniel right now.'" That was the exact time Daniel and I had been sitting on the cinder-block window ledge at two in the morning. Daniel was thrilled, and from then on, he no longer walked with his head down.

Back in the present, I hurriedly asked my cell mates, "Where is Cina?" I wanted to formally hand off the nightly jailhouse services in our cell, along with my bag filled with nearly two hundred dollars' worth of ramen noodles, cigarettes, Snickers bars, toothpaste, toothbrushes, bars of soap, and small containers of shampoos for Cina to share with the guys at our after-service fellowship. We had discussed the transition during our nightly midnight Jericho-style prayer walks around the perimeter of Cell Block #5.

The guards were standing outside my cell, ready to escort me to my release. "Who *faraje* [freed] you?" they asked.

Each time a prisoner was released, the guards and the entire cell block would begin chanting the prisoner's nationality and the Arabic word that meant, "You "re free." Hence the chant: "*Amérique faraje!*"

Many times, during my imprisonment, I had been asked if Jason Bourne was going to arrive in a helicopter along with President Obama to extract me. The prison was several stories high with an inner courtyard. From each floor, we could stand at the open-air cinder-block windows and look down. The cell mates would point up jokingly at the night sky and say,

"Tonight, my friend," as their arm would circle, making the motion of the rotors of the helicopter, pretending it was lowering into the courtyard to extract me in a clandestine international special-ops mission.

And so the question was asked by the guards as I was escorted down the long corridor toward the warden's office: "Who *faraje Amérique?*"

I kept repeating, "American Embassy is waiting for my call that I'm released."

Into another ratchet van I went, to be transported to a modular building some distance away from the main prison. When we arrived, the officers there were scrambling to find the paperwork authorizing my release. I was seated for some time in a waiting area, until I finally approached the counter and requested to speak to one of the officers. When a woman came over, I explained that I had been "*farajed*" and that American Embassy was waiting for my direct call to my country's ambassador. She returned to the back of the office area, where I could see a group of about seven officers conferring, then looking my way. The woman returned to the counter and said, "Mr. David, we have no paperwork for your release. Who *farajed* you?"

I replied, "Madame, please expedite this immediately. My embassy is waiting for the confirmation of my release."

She suddenly produced a blue, triplicate, old-school carbon-type piece of paper from a folder and instructed me to leave. I asked her to write in English and Arabic that I had been "*farajed*" and to also include her name and contact information. She leaned over and quietly said, "Mr. David, that is not allowed. You can call the court later about your case."

I was handed my cell phone and the cash I'd had in my pocket when I entered the prison. My phone turned on with a 23 percent battery charge left. I guess it was a representation of heaven's battery charge for the duration of my twenty-three days in prison. Twenty-three percent was more than enough to call my wife to tell her I had been released. When she answered and I told her the good news, I immediately heard shouts, applause, and cries of "Thank You, Jesus!" from the group of teachers who had faithfully surrounded my wife during our ordeal.

"Honey, I'm in the taxi on my way home!"

Three Years Later: Napa Valley, California. It was late at night as I walked around our living room in Northern California. I was pacing and pondering. The song playing in the background, "Through It All," by Darlene Zschech, had always been one of my favorites. Tears streamed down my face, just as they had on my first day in the maximum-security prison while my cell mate sang that very song in Cell #5, Block #10. I had been so exhausted by the shackles of shame. Maybe it was my own lack of identity with Christ. I could sense the hushed whispers of judgment and the unspoken questions from relatives, friends, and longtime church acquaintances: *So, what did he* really *do? Why was he* really *locked up abroad?* The time had come to fully accept my release from the shackles of shame. In reality, I had been set free long before I ever set foot on the hot Arabian sand of Abu Dhabi. But I had allowed the quiet voices of judgment to define me and cloak me in shame. I sobbed uncontrollably as I released the fear and shame of what everyone expected from me and what they might have thought of me and our family. I embraced my freedom and identity in Christ, accepting that I had been set free over two thousand years ago. I had been willing to go behind bars to complete an undercover rescue mission for over twenty men from Latin

America, Russia, the Philippines, Nigeria, South Africa, Uganda, Pakistan, India, Bangladesh, and the United Kingdom. My King's mission assignment: "International Arms Dealer: One willing Christian, needed to go into a maximum-security prison and share the Gospel with twenty-three men who had lost their way and who needed redemption. Tats not required, but optional."

ABOUT DAVID SAUCEDA

David, an educator for over twenty years, has a passion for helping good schools become great schools. He and his wife Nanette, also an educator, have been fortunate enough to work in education globally in public, private and charter school environments in Illinois, California, Hawaii and overseas in Abu Dhabi. David has a master's degree in Curriculum and Instruction. He was selected to participate in Harvard's Principal Leadership program with other leaders from over 120 countries. David, Nanette and their two young adult kids, 8 designer chickens and their 2 dogs live in the beautiful Napa Valley in California. They currently serve their respective school communities, serve in their local church, and have been AirBNB Super-host for the past several years in their beautiful Hacienda de Paz.

https://www.instagram.com/donsauceda

6

RISK MORE, REFLECT MORE, AND DO MORE THAT WILL LIVE ON!

BY BOBBY JONES

Delight yourself also in the LORD, and He shall give you the desires of your heart. —Psalm 37:4 NKJV

For as long as I can remember, I have wanted all that God has for me. I have always had zero "quit" in me. I am not sure that anyone besides me knows how much that is true. I do not allow myself to be beat consistently or to stay down when I am knocked down. I do not believe that anything good grows out of comfort. I believe that God has every intention for each one of us to live a life of significance. We only have one life. We all have different hurdles and adversities to overcome, but the journey is what makes our lives so special. Life is extremely short. If we don't take immediate action in our lives, then we can quickly be left with the regrets of a life unfulfilled and of words left unspoken.

My best friend, Matthew, called my house one day in the summer of 1984. I remember clearly my stepfather answering the call on an old black-and-gold rotary telephone. I was five years old. Matthew had called me to ask if I wanted to play football. I said "yes" while instinctively stepping out of my comfort zone. This one decision at that tender young age helped to shape my life and was the beginning of the building of character I would need later in life. I remember the first time I put my cleats on and the smell of the freshly cut grass of the baseball field, as I walked toward right field at the start of my first practice. My life was changed from that day forward.

Today, I know I was extremely fortunate when my parents separated in 1981, that both my mother and father would remarry. From the age of two, I would forever have two mothers and two fathers. I think that too often, we are searching for the "perfect" life in this filtered world. For me, it was the perfect world in which my mother and father had never divorced. However, God can take anything and use it for our good—and not only for our good, but He can make it better than we ever imagine if we trust that His will is always good. In this case, as always, God knew exactly what He was doing. God, of course, is omnipresent. He also knows the end from the beginning.

Both of my fathers were very tough on me—in a good way. My biological father would wake me up at 5 a.m. to be at summer workouts by 6 a.m. He would often say early in the morning, "Get up—you are not going to lie around the house all day!" My stepfather was my first head coach, and he was harder on me than anyone else on the team. He would yell at me to the point that I burst into tears on the field, because he knew that was when I was at my best.

I always wanted to be the best at everything I did for both of my fathers. Both men taught me how to be a man of my word. My dad taught me to be extremely detail-oriented. Not one thing could ever be out of order. It was unacceptable. He taught me this out of love, and I know it is true because he tells me all the time that he loves me. My stepfather taught me how to be humble and that actions speak louder than words. He has always treated me just like his own son. I was taught the fundamentals I needed in sports, and they both also taught me the fundamentals of life.

My mother is so giving that it is almost to a fault. Her life has been made up of sacrifices for her children. I am the oldest of three siblings—two girls and a boy—on my mom's side of the family, and I am the oldest of three brothers on my dad's side. When she was younger, Mom was an extremely talented student, but she put her dreams of working in the medical field on hold for her children. Her heart of gold is unmatched by anyone's that I know.

My stepmother lived through great adversity at a young age. Both of her parents died in her arms, and she put herself through college after being raised in an orphanage. Still, she never made excuses, and she has always been giving and supportive of all her children. She never treated me as anything less than her own.

My mother taught me that nothing matters more than to love God, family, and friends. My stepmother is an extremely talented cook, and she also taught me at an early age to be wise with my money and to be a good steward of it.

If you believe in yourself and have dedication and pride—and never quit—you'll be a winner. The price of victory is high, but so are the rewards." —Bear Bryant

This is a quote that I live by in many ways. I believe that by believing that God is in control of everything and by believing in myself and never quitting, anything is possible. Whether you believe God is in control or not, still does not change the fact that He is. If you do not believe in yourself, then how can anyone else? I believed that while I was playing baseball, I was the fastest kid in the park...and I was. I stole every base, and I was never thrown out. I had other fast kids challenge me to a race, and I would be at home plate starting from the fence, in center field, before they could get to the infield.

As an adult, I believed I could raise millions of dollars to buy real estate, and I did. Whatever I have ever wanted, I have believed I could get it, and with God as my starting point, I have always obtained it. A life of not believing in God or in yourself is extremely unfulfilling. God is always waiting for us to take action so that He can move in our lives.

All I ever wanted to do in my youth was to play sports and eventually play college football. I played both football and baseball from the age of five, and in high school, I played football, baseball, and basketball and I ran on the track team. For the most part, I was a good kid and stayed out of trouble. I was extremely fortunate to be raised in church. I went to a Methodist church on my mother's side, a Baptist church on the weekends spent on my father's side, and I attended a Catholic elementary school. The foundation my parents chose to give me prepared me and gave me the strength and discernment to overcome spiritual battles later in life.

Our adversary is extremely crafty. He is the father of all lies, and a good liar can make a lie sound so sweet, just like the truth. The enemy is the best liar there is. It is extremely hard to recognize his lies when you are not consistently spending time with God. When I was thirteen years of age, I realized very quickly that I had the ability to charm girls better than most. It came extremely easy to me. I met a girl I will call Jennifer. She was eighteen years old, a varsity cheerleader. I was only thirteen when she introduced me to what would soon become a sexual addiction, with the inability or desire to commit to anyone. It never occurred to me at the time that I was doing anything wrong. I reasoned that I was not married, and I thought that by being single I was not accountable to anyone.

When I was fourteen years old, I met my oldest son's mother. I met her while I was on a double date with her best friend at the time. She was beautiful, and we were immediately attracted to one another. We dated for the next four and a half years.

In the spring of 1997, I was given the opportunity I had dreamed about for so many years. My parents took me to visit the college football coach whom my stepfather had played for many years before. It was a long drive there, and the whole time I knew I was carrying a secret. Paige, my oldest son's mother, had called me a few weeks before and told me she was pregnant.

It was a beautiful day. My mother was so proud as we explored an art scholarship possibility and as we spoke to the head football coach about playing for his championship college football team. Needless to say, it was an even longer ride home. I tried to pretend I was happy in that moment. However, my heart was heavy because I was struggling to find the right time to tell my parents about the pregnancy.

My mother left work crying the day I finally told her over the phone. She was upset because she had no idea what decisions I had been making. I asked her how this would affect my ability to play college football, and she told me I would have to work to care for my child and that college and football were no longer in the equation. And so working is exactly what I did—and to be honest, I did it with heavy resentment. I became a workaholic, working three jobs a day. One summer I worked as a lifeguard in the mornings, at a sporting goods store in the evenings, and overnight I stocked the retail store my mother managed. I worked out equally as hard between shifts at my cousin's gym, and I slept the best I could on my lunch hour overnight at work.

I was not a good father in the early years of my first son, Jackson's life. During that time, cell phones had just recently become popular, and out of sight was out of mind in many ways for me. I fell deeper and deeper into meaningless relationships. There were many women I would have been extremely lucky to have had a stable relationship or even marriage with, but I could not be faithful. All I did was work, work out, and date as many women as possible.

By allowing this flaw in my life to casually hang around, I was very vulnerable. The enemy will take your weaknesses and drag you down a rabbit hole you never thought possible if you allow him to do so. When I was twenty-one years old, I met a girl whom I will leave unnamed that my father knew was not right for me. I most likely was not right for her, either, at the time. She was fun and exciting, and she was different from the others.

Another big problem with dating so many different people is that you start building an image of the perfect person in your mind. I would say to myself that one girl did not have the personality that a previous girl had had, or that my conversations with another girl weren't as deep as they were with someone else. I would also tell myself I was not attracted to one girl as another. On and on the cycle continued. I would always start over with a different chase because the new conversations and encounters were exciting, but then I would get bored. This new girl, though—she was fun, exciting, and different from everyone else.

I began to hang around with the wrong people by associating with this girl. In a few situations, loaded guns were put in my face. I was hanging out with people who held others up at gunpoint. I was in many physical fights, and I started to live with a very unstable drug dealer. She and I both developed a serious drug problem. I was still working three jobs, but I began to see how much money my roommate was making by selling drugs.

It is not necessary to go into how involved in that lifestyle I became. A little drop of poison in your drink can still be deadly. It does not always matter what your level of involvement is. The bottom line is that I was not innocent in my actions. After many close circumstances that could have landed me in prison, I finally stopped doing drugs cold turkey. I do not know anyone else who could have stopped at that point without going to rehab. I could not have stopped, either, without the belief that God overcomes all and with the belief in myself that I had had from an early age.

By the age of twenty-three, I had become heavily involved in real estate. I acquired a lot of money between the ages of twenty-three and twenty-nine. But then I slipped back into my old ways with women. I had a home in a very desirable area. I also had a beach house, drove a BMW, and wore a Rolex watch. I was "that guy." I would fly a professional football cheerleader across the country to spend time with her just because I could. I was living a very materialistic lifestyle.

Then I met another woman who somehow convinced me to marry her after five months. We were married only ten months, from June 2008 until April of 2009. During that time, the market crashed at the end of 2008, and I lost everything virtually overnight. I lost my wife, three personal houses, including my beach home, all my investment properties, all my money, and nearly all my possessions in the divorce.

Our marriage did not have a strong foundation. We barely knew one another. We did attend church together. The last day we spent together was Easter Sunday of 2009. I was singing and leading worship at church that morning, but she never made it to church. I told her that day that we should attend counseling. I even tried to save the marriage by attending counseling without her. She never showed up. It all happened so fast. I am not sure either one of us really knew why we divorced.

Now I had come from extreme lows in my life to extreme highs, and now again back down to an extremely low point. I had not had any additional business come in for several months. I was struggling. I remember walking back into church and sitting where I used to sit with my wife. I thought of all the material things that we used to own together. Now I sat there with roughly twenty dollars to my name.

That day, I remember telling God that I did not have anything left, but that I would give Him all I had. I put all of my money in the offering and walked out of the church with a feeling of hope, because I knew I was at the point I wanted to go all-in with God. The very next week, I received thousands of dollars in business it. I knew there was only one way to explain it.

Since that day, I have put my heart into becoming a good father. I am teaching my boys the fundamentals that I was taught as a child. I am also raising them in church to be men of God. God gave me something so much better than football with my first son, Jackson. God's way for us is always better. Even when we begin with poor decisions, He always has another path back to allow us to receive all He has for us.

Soon I became a music worship leader again, and now I have, for many years, attended the main campus of Church of the Highlands. It is one of the largest churches in the world. I have the honor of being involved with the church leadership, and my pastor, Chris Hodges, has a calling on his life that surpasses words. His leadership as a pastor has been paramount to my life and success.

Matthew, my childhood best friend who called me at five years old and changed my life by introducing me to football, has since been legally declared dead. He and his girlfriend went out on a boating trip in the Gulf of Mexico on a day that appeared to have pleasant weather. But the weather conditions quickly changed, the boat was found capsized, and their bodies were never found. Decisions we make can often lead us to a place that we never thought they would take us in the beginning. I often wonder why God took Matthew home and still has a plan here on this earth for me.

I do not want to waste my life. I want to be someone who risks more. I want to get out of my comfort zone and trust God. I want to step out in faith every single day and rely on Him to catch me and carry me the rest of the way. I want to be someone who reflects more. I want to stop and appreciate the things that God has given me. I want to be grateful for my family, my friends, my talents, and the lessons I have learned… and not take one thing for granted. I want to do more that will live on in the lives of others. I want this chapter I have written to reach people whom I may never see. I want to teach a kid how to swing a bat or help someone financially who would never ask for it. I have the same desires for each of you.

The concept for this chapter was inspired by a sermon by Tony Campolo, a sociology professor and well-known Christian speaker. He described a study of fifty people over the age of ninety-five who were asked what they would do differently if given the opportunity to live life over again. The study revealed that their desires were to risk more, reflect more, and do more that would live on in the lives of others.

As I complete this chapter, I have been on a plane, in airports, and in hotels during my honeymoon following my beautiful wedding a few days ago... I realize all over again that God is good all the time and His timing is always perfect. I have become a man who desires to be in a committed relationship. I am committed to God first, and then to my wife, Rosie; my three beautiful sons: Jackson, Justin, and Jordan; and the rest of my family, and finally to my legacy and to the world. I believe that all good things come from an uphill climb. My prayer is that you will keep looking for the next challenge, the next goal to achieve, and the next mountain to climb.

Think BIG because nothing is too big for our God. Believe in Him and believe in yourself.

ABOUT BOBBY JONES

Bobby Jones was born and raised in Birmingham, Alabama. A talented athlete and artist that, like many, allowed the enemy to drag his life down a rabbit hole, through subtle temptations, to the brink of total destruction. Today, by the grace of God, he is a successful Real Estate entrepreneur, author, and well-known public figure in Alabama as well as nationally. In this chapter you will see that it is never too late to go back to the fundamentals. It is never too late to allow God to be first in our life and it is never too late to live out the purpose and calling that God has waiting for us.

Bobby Jones is also a Real Estate expert, investor and entrepreneur. Bobby has built multiple successful Real Estate companies. Bobby strives to give value to others and has done so through multiple social media and church platforms. Bobby believes he is called to be a leader. A former music worship leader, Bobby currently helps lead as a dream team member for, Church of the Highlands, one of the largest Church organizations in the country. Bobby leads and is a member of multiple Real Estate Investor Associations and masterminds.

When Bobby is not working or writing, he enjoys spending time with his family inclusive of his wife Rosie and his three son's Jackson, Justin and Jordan. Bobby also enjoys working out, reading, artwork, playing sports, mixed martial arts, song writing, singing and playing the piano and guitar.

Believing that all good things come from an uphill climb and from outside our comfort zone... Bobby is always looking for the next challenge, the next goal to achieve and the next mountain to climb.

https://www.instagram.com/fementrepreneur

bobby.jones@yellowhammerproperties.com

7

LIVING FROM THE SPIRIT
BY BRICE TABOR

Growing up as a pastor's kid, I was well versed in the ways of the church. At a very early age, I had the religious practices of being a Christian down pretty well. But having religious practice and having a relationship with Jesus are two totally different things. Entering junior high, I found myself with the challenge of trying to experience as much of the world as possible while still making it to heaven when I die. What a foolish way to live! I was spiritually declining the best party and feast ever, choosing instead the garbage in the alley dumpster.

I lived several years like this, but through the influence of some friends' radical encounters with Jesus, I eventually found myself in a pool of tears after being touched by the power and love of Jesus. God saved me and set me on fire. I started taking my Bible to school, telling all my friends about Jesus, making tracts on receipt paper to hand out to customers while working at Taco Bell. (Yes, I worked there. Yes, handing out tracts almost got me fired, and, yes, believe it or not, I still eat there!) I was spending hours a day in my Bible and in prayer. My life got flipped upside down. But really, it got flipped right side up.

However, as time progressed, my passion and fire turned into a slow simmer. I had developed a thorough understanding of God's Word, but I didn't seem to have the same revelatory rush I once got when I read the Bible. I was searching different interpretations of Scripture and looking for different preachers' perspectives on the Bible. But I just couldn't find the same excitement that I had when I encountered my First Love. That and the cares of this world were totally choking out the Word that had been planted in my heart. On the outside, things were going pretty well. I had a beautiful wife, a nice house, great kids, a good job. But inside, I felt so empty.

One day, I went to my office to fulfill the obligatory rule of "spending time with God." I apathetically opened my Bible and began to read. After reading a few verses, I stopped. My long, slow regression of no longer being "Coco for Cocoa Puffs" about Jesus had caught up to me. "Why don't I really care anymore?" I asked the Lord. "I'd rather be reading Kansas City Chiefs articles or getting other things accomplished." I continued, "I know the problem isn't with You, but with me. Please help me."

And He did. That moment marked a major turning point in my life. Jesus began to teach me things in the Spirit through the Word that I hadn't been able to see before, truths that helped me live a sustainable lifestyle with God that wasn't driven by me or my abilities. With that, let's begin with some of these truths.

God Tabernacles with Men

Most believers are aware that the Old Testament temple was the place where God would come and dwell with the assigned priest on behalf of the people. But what many believers are unaware of is that the functionality and layout of the Old Testament temple are essential to understanding how we as the New Testament temples of God operate. Hebrews 8:5 (TPT) says, "The priests on earth serve in a temple that is but a copy modeled after the heavenly sanctuary; a shadow of the reality."

What exactly does this verse mean when it mentions "modeled after the heavenly sanctuary"? In the unseen dimension of the Spirit, is there a heavenly sanctuary to the exact specifications that were given to Moses? I can't help but think the answer is yes, because that's what Scripture says in plain form. However, Jesus' claim to be the temple of God makes it difficult to conclude that He isn't the most true and pure model of the heavenly sanctuary. Furthermore, according to Revelation 21, in the end God (in the Greek *"Theos,"* meaning "Father, Son, and Holy Spirit") will tabernacle with men. God tabernacling with men is and is continually manifesting to be the new heaven and new earth. So, it's possible to conclude that man has always been the designed heavenly sanctuary—not necessarily a spiritual "building" in the way we understand a building to be in the natural.

The point in saying all of this is that God the Holy Spirit now resides in men through our faith in the Son of God, Jesus Christ. We are the heavenly tabernacles. We are the ultimate and true design of the tabernacle of God. And as the tabernacle of God, there is a designed flow of the Spirit through us that we can easily access and naturally experience.

The Temple Layout

The basic layout and functionality of the temple in the Old Testament is made up of three areas: the outer courts, the Holy Place, and the Holy of Holies. Priests would begin their priestly duties in the outer courts and then progress into the Holy Place and after that, the Holy of Holies. One of the most important parallels that we can make when comparing the Old Testament temple and the New Testament temple are these three dimensions. The outer courts in the New Testament is the human body. The Holy Place in the New Testament is a human soul. The Holy of Holies in the New Testament is the human spirit. Here is a diagram to help illustrate this concept:

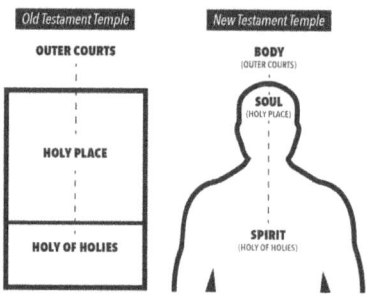

The River Begins in Our Bellies

The Old Testament priestly ministry was one that worked from the outside in. The priests began in the outer courts and progressed inward by following the necessary procedures. However, through Christ, the priestly ministry has reversed. There is no longer any need to progress inward through rules or procedures. The veil was torn open for all to access and abide within the Father through Spirit-to-spirit union. We are seated with Christ in heavenly places, and according to Hebrews 12, we have already come to Mount Zion, the festal gathering of angels, the saints made perfect, the Judge, and Jesus. The gift of the Holy Spirit has created a totally new and heavenly existence in us. Our reality is now one with Christ.

Our unionized spirit with Christ's Spirit is who we are. We no longer live, but it is Christ who lives in us. This is where life begins for believers. The challenge, which is really no challenge at all, is learning how to cause the River of Life to bubble up from our Holy of Holies and into our Holy Place. Look no further than John 7:38 (Literal Standard Version) for our instructions. This verslays, "...he who is believing in Me, according as the Writing said, Rivers of living water will flow out Ihis belly..."

That's it. It's so simple that most people miss it. Surely it can't be that easy, right? Let me break it down a bit. Actively believing in Jesus causes living water to bubble up and out of our innermost being. No works are welcome here. In the place of drinking from the Wellspring of Life, nothing we can add is adequate or appropriate. Believing in Jesus is the only requirement. Faith in Jesus is far more than salvation from the Second Death—it's the key to living within Abundant Life itself. It's the only way to cause our new existence to bubble up and flow into the other faculties of our temples.

Get Out of Your Mind

Our intellect has a very hard time perceiving spiritual realities. And this is commonly what we believers try to do. Our intellect is like our taste buds. Our taste buds are prone to losing interest in certain tastes and flavors. If we turn the word into knowledge, our minds will become bored eventually, just like our taste buds become bored with the same foods. However, if we approach the Word as spiritual sustenance for our bellies, then it's a totally different story. Our bellies don't care if they've had the same meal—they just want the sustenance and nutrients! This is how we should approach the Word of God—as sustenance, not as knowledge; as food, not as something to be learned.

If we are approaching a relationship with God through our intellect rather than through our spirit, we will eventually find ourselves running into problems. It's like when a car is sitting still but the air-conditioner is on. Pretty soon, the air is no longer cool. You can crank the thermostat as cold as you want to, but if that engine isn't engaged and delivering power, the A/C won't produce cold air.

Getting out of your mind is done simply by believing. Anything that you want to experience from the unseen realm must be accessed by faith. Believing is how we cause the unseen realm to manifest into the seen realm. This is why Jesus says, "Believe in me so that Rivers of Living Water will flow out from your innermost being." The mind is incapable of creating the nutrients of God by itself. Our minds must get the heavenly nutrients they need from Spirit-to-spirit union with Christ; through faith and faith alone.

To Perceive Him We Must Eat and Drink Him

The King is not inviting us to a classroom. He is inviting us to a feast. We are to "Let joy be [our] continual feast" (1 Thessalonians 5:16 TPT). Jesus shouted to the crowds, "Come to Me all who are thirsty!" He says, "He who eats My flesh and drinks My blood has eternal life." And He says "This is the blood of My covenant. Take and drink. This is My body, broken for you. Take and eat."

Do you truly want to learn from God? Do you want a relationship that is vibrant and alive? Then enjoy Him! Eat and drink the pleasures of Him and His life. There is no other way to truly grow in Christ. Wisdom itself even says, "She has slaughtered her meat, she has mixed her wine, she has also furnished her table. She has sent out her maidens, she cries out from the highest places of the city, 'Whoever is simple, let him turn in here!' As for him who lacks understanding, she says to him, 'Come, eat of my bread and drink of the wine I have mixed'" (Proverbs 9:2–5 NKJV).

What I've described are the fundamentals to growing more spiritual in Christ. The Father is seeking those who will worship Him this way. He is after those who will worship Him in Spirit and in truth. It's essential to understand that it has nothing to do with our understanding. It has nothing to do with us at all. For us to grow in Him, we simply engage the engine of the Spirit by faith in Jesus. The River of Life bubbles up into our minds, and we experience the nature of heaven through this union. This is truly the work of God. Our entire being is flooded with light through faith in Jesus so that everywhere we go, we release the nature of Christ through our bodies. This is the New Testament priestly progression: Union with Christ in the Holy of Holies. The flooding of Christ into our Holy Place. The pouring out of Christ into the outer courts of our bodies.

ABOUT BRICE TABOR

Brice Tabor is a husband, father of four, and pastor from Wichita, Kansas. He is passionate about helping others experience the joys and freedoms that come from knowing Jesus Christ.

Through the faithful shepherding of Jesus, Brice Tabor has learned how to access the presence of God in spirit and truth so that the river of life can naturally flow through every area of his life. Unfortunately, many believers feel stuck and bored in their walks with God, and Brice was no different. However, with some simple revelations from the Lord, he has discovered how to regularly experience the riches of knowing Christ and partake in the pleasures that come from communion with Him.

https://www.instagram.com/bricetabor

8

A SIT-DOWN WITH MR. BIG

BY DEREK TYE

So, here was my big chance. You know, the kind of chance that only comes around once in a lifetime. I had been given a thirty-minute interview with one of the richest and most powerful people on the planet. The time had been approved. The schedule was set. The anticipation had mounted. One day to go now... If you had one chance to ask the "big" questions to a super-successful individual, and you knew that one of those answers could change your life, you would take it pretty seriously too!

Being a prepared person, I found myself overanalyzing the questions I would ask. Who would be the beneficiaries of these questions and answers? Was it me, was it my family, or was it Mr. Big? Well, if you could put yourself in my situation, you would ask yourself the same things. So, I made the decision that I was definitely *not* going to waste Mr. Big's time or my own. I carefully crafted each question and even threw in a few bonus questions just in case I ran out of questions before we ran out of time. I had heard that Mr. Big was very efficient and did not like to ramble.

Fast-forward to the big day. One hour before the interview, I submitted the questions to Mr. Big's handler. She took my list like it was a manifesto, then she removed herself to another room, and I waited. Here are the questions I had come up with:

- What is your secret to success?
- If you had to start over again today, what would you do?
- Do you think education is worthwhile?
- What is life's most important lesson?
- What should I put first before everything else?
- How do you structure your day to make every moment count?

Mr. Big's handler came back into the room with a disappointed look on her face. Now I was getting really nervous. She explained, "Mr. Big has already answered each and every one of these questions in magazine, television, podcast, book, and YouTube interviews. Since he is extremely busy and only likes to answer questions once, he is cancelling your interview today. He has summarized all of these answers in addition to hundreds of other answers in this one book." She handed me a small book and walked away. More on that later.

I was shocked. Dumbfounded, disappointed, and upset. How would *you* feel? *I have squandered my one big chance*, I thought. *What will I do now?*

This story is not real. Shocking, right? But this is a scenario that has played out hundreds of times in my life. Whenever I start to follow a guru or an expert on a certain subject matter, I start to build up that person's value in my mind. I do this to the point that I develop a fascination with that person and obsess over how getting advice directly from them could somehow change my life. I then start reading all their books, watching all their interviews, and doing all the research I can on the person. When I have exhausted those possibilities, I still have questions. So, I started creating a list of the questions I would ask someone in case I was ever able to meet them in person. The truth is, most of us don't do this with the "smartest person ever," both past or present: the Creator of the universe. Or at least, I haven't been doing this like I should.

In Matthew 6:33, we are told to seek FIRST His Kingdom and His righteousness, and then all these other things will be added to us. So, what are these "other things"? Money, power, influence, relationships, health, business success, and personal enjoyment we can't even imagine. So, who is the "He" in the verse? It is God, the Creator of all life. We are to seek Him first in everything we do. So, now I am going to share with you some practical ways to seek God's Kingdom first, and then we can see what can happen in your life. This will result in a much better story even than interviewing "Mr. Big."

So, let's imagine in the story I started with that Mr. Big was really God Himself. He is sitting in heaven, waiting for His sons and daughters, those people who love Him and are called according to His purpose, to simply seek Him and to ask Him questions: Small questions and big, burning questions. Questions to help us decide what to eat for lunch or what will be the next billion-dollar business. Questions about how to remove hunger or violence from the world.

How many people actually do present these types of questions to God? How many people take the time to pray every day, to read the Bible, to meditate on His words, and to talk to other believers about Him? I don't know the numbers or the percentages, but I do know there are a lot of people who do everything but seek God. They still seek out self-help books, television stars, YouTube broadcasters, self-improvement seminars, yoga, psychologists, psychics, yogis, crystal balls, tea leaves, palm readers, and all kinds of other false resources.

So, if you are given the opportunity to ask God Himself to help you with the answers to the big, burning questions of life, start by figuring out what you really want to know. Is your list similar to mine at the beginning of this chapter? What are your burning questions? If you don't have a list, what would your list look like? Go ahead and write down your list now...

Now that you have your starting list, where will you go to seek this information? It is really hard to have a sit-down conversation with God and feel like you are getting clear, even audible, answers—I haven't had that experience yet myself—so what else can you do? Personally, I start by reading the Bible. I have read the Bible through about four times now during my lifetime thus far. Each time I read it, I get new information, revelation, and understanding. My goal over the last few years has been to read it from cover to cover in one year. This is aggressive, but I am still working on it.

There is an old saying: Each time you go to the same spot at a river, you are a different man and it is a different river. Well, the Word of God doesn't change, but we certainly do. If you learn anything from this chapter, I hope you pick up on the infinite knowledge available to you through reading the Bible. You cannot hope to get enough from it by listening to the pastor read a few passages on Sunday at church. You really need to own the pursuit of the Word and challenge yourself to read it every day. That is where the Kingdom experience begins: with knowing what is in the Bible and where to find it. And that is a journey! It does not happen overnight. It is a lifetime journey.

You may be saying, "Derek, I don't have that kind of time or energy." Well, you have to start somewhere! I would ask God and the Holy Spirit to help you to know where to begin. And ask the Holy Spirit to show you specific passages, chapters, or places to learn from. When you become consistent about this pursuit, you will see your Kingdom experience increase.

Once you find yourself regularly pursuing God's Word, ask the Holy Spirit to help translate what you are reading into practical action steps for your life. Ask Him to help you remember what you read. Ask Him to show you current situations in the context of what you are reading. This is one of the best ways to make the Bible more interesting than just words on a paper.

The next step is to get to know God intimately. The way I do this is to read about His heart for me. You can read both Scripture and great books about God. I would also read the other chapters in this book to gain different Kingdom-minded authors' perspectives on this. God does have a heart for you. He cares for you. He wants you to succeed and prosper. He wants to expand His Kingdom here on the earth. One of my all-time favorite authors is Myles Munroe. He has written several books about God's heart for us and about the Kingdom. Please do yourself a favor, and after you have read this book, watch his videos on YouTube or read one of his amazing books. It will change your perspective.

I also like to pray and ask God to specifically reveal His heart to me. I start by praising Him for what He has already done. I ask Him to show me anything I need to reconcile in my life. I specifically have petitions that I present to God every day. Specifically, I ask for Him to help me with my relationship with my wife, with my five kids, in my businesses, with my friends and extended family, with my home and country, and in my health. I also ask Him to help me to expand the Kingdom every day.

In addition, I ask the Holy Spirit to constantly talk to me, to reveal to me His secrets. I am working on this daily, and I hope to continue to hear that still, small voice that God likes to speak with. I see a lot of value in getting quiet with Him! Over the last 17 years our business has been pretty successful according to most people's standards. My wife and I have started up 10 businesses, and a few of them are still around making money. Our most successful business has been selling real estate in the Greater Cincinnati area since 2004. As of the time of this writing, we have sold about 1,430 homes for over $330,000,000 in sales volume. This has been a great financial blessing to our family and to the team members we have worked with over the years. We have also been able to take the excess funds from the real estate and start other businesses. Like I said earlier, we actually still have a few open for business. Our next most financially prosperous business has been our real estate rental portfolio. We have owned up to five luxury short-term rental properties in Ohio. We recently sold a two-family property and are now down to three. These have also been a big blessing to us.

Along the way, we have also had our fair share of large business losses as well. One particular business failure involved about three years of my time and almost $100,000 of our profits from our other companies on a technology startup. Another business side venture cost me three years, and we barely broke even. Another business loss cost us about ten thousand dollars and about six months of our time. There are several others that I could recount that had different financial and time losses. What is the point? As we ask the ultimate business Advice Giver on what action to take, sometimes we get it wrong. We may not ask, we may not listen, or we just may not hear Him correctly. I like to think of the words of Romans 8:28 (NIV):

And we know that in all things God works for the good of those who love him, who have been called according to his purpose.

So, God is always working things out for those who love Him. My number-one job has to be to love Him first, and then He can work out some of this junk and some of these scenarios that I find myself in. One of the redeeming thoughts I have is that God is often protecting me from even bigger investment losses. Or sometimes I think the devil gives us success in this world in the wrong pursuits, just to keep us from doing what God really wants us to do. In that vein, if God shut down some of my business ventures, it was probably a blessing, because I could have been successful in any of those business ideas and I might not be here today where I am. I am at peace, I have great relationships, I have my health, and I can spend most of my days doing things that I love to do, as opposed to working for companies or people that I don't really like. Thank You, God!

Finally, know that pursuing wealth, success, and financial freedom is not the point. The point is to pursue God with all that you do, and He will add all of these other things to your life—if you are ready for them. It took me twenty years to see this, but I can tell you it was worth the wait. In some ways, I have barely scratched the surface of financial wealth. In other areas, I feel rich beyond what I could have ever dreamed of. The key isn't the number in my bank account or the net worth number at the bottom of my personal financial statement. It is the relationship and right standing I have with the Creator of the universe, my Daddy, my Abba Father. This is real wealth!

So, as you are formulating your next move, whether it is personal or for a new business venture, I want you to keep some of these tips in mind: 1. Pursue God and His Kingdom first. 2. Read your Bible regularly. 3. Ask the Holy Spirit to show you specific passages of Scripture that apply to your situation. 4. Ask the Holy Spirit to show you His heart for you and for others. 5. Ask the Holy Spirit to show you His business secrets and how to redeem your past failures. 6. Stay in an intimate relationship with God and talk to Him all day long!

I will leave you with this: In all things, pursue God first. He will richly bless you and your family. He will show you true contentment and satisfaction. And I will be praying for you in your journey!

Derek Tye's personal mission statement is to build, inspire, and love people to live up to their God-given calling and live life to the fullest. He has achieved success in the real estate business and would love to share his strategies with other real estate agents. After selling over 1,430 homes with over $330,000,000 in volume and spending over $1,000,000 on his own real estate sales business, he can also tell you what *not* to do! He is also still running his own sales team, The Tye Group, in Cincinnati, Ohio, and he enjoys offering agents relevant strategies to help them achieve breakthrough in both life and business.

ABOUT DEREK TYE

My name is Derek Tye. My personal Mission Statement is too build, inspire and love people to live up to their God-given calling and live life to the fullest. I have achieved success in the real estate business and would love to share strategies with you. After selling over 1,400 homes and spending over $1,000,000 on my own real estate sales business I can tell you what NOT to do! I am still running my own sales team and will be offering you relevant strategies to help you achieve breakthrough in both life and business.

My greatest accomplishments are not found in the real estate business, though. I am grateful for the career I have as a Realtor. However, my first love is God, then my beautiful wife since 1996, my 5 kids, and my awesome friends. I also love to hike, play volleyball and ride my mountain bike. I enjoy playing around on our hobby farm too. I am also a real estate investor so I put my money where my mouth is and own several short term rental homes!

https://instagram.com/thattyeguy

www.derektye.com

9

THE STRUGGLE IS REAL

BY J.D. JUAREZ

Don't Let Your Struggle Become Your Identity! To *struggle* is defined as "to make forceful or violent efforts to get free of restraint or constriction" (*Oxford Languages*). When I think of the word *struggle*, what comes to my mind is another word for *quitting*. So many times, over and over I said to myself, "I just want to quit." I just wanted to die because the struggle got so severe it became painful to even endure, and it constricted me from moving forward. In other words, I lost hope, but if the truth be told, we all have all had those types of days. We can see here a reference in Scripture:

"Is not all human life a struggle? Our lives are like that of a hired hand, like a worker who longs for the shade, like a servant waiting to be paid. I, too, have been assigned months of futility, long and weary nights of misery. Lying in bed, I think, 'When will it be morning?' But the night drags on, and I toss till dawn. My body is covered with maggots and scabs. My skin breaks open, oozing with pus." —Job 7:1–5 NLT

We see here a man who had lost his wealth, his family, and even his dignity. I can imagine Job was sitting and probably thinking, *What in the world did I do?* He was facing some of the harshest pain that anyone can face, and like many people, he wanted answers. We see here in Scripture that he cried out to God because life didn't make sense to him anymore. To be honest, Job had every right to be mad, but one thing I do see that is very key is that he did not curse God and die, as his friends told him to do. Little did he know, God was about to use this situation to elevate, bless, and promote Job.

I realized throughout this story I cannot let my struggles define me in who I was or where I am destined to go. You read the quote above: "Don't let your struggle become your identity." The reality is that when we come to this conclusion of wanting to quit or give up, it's often because we are exhausted. We once had a vision and there was a purpose behind it that drove us to reach great lengths to get there. Somewhere down the road, however, something came along and brought conflict, took something from us, shamed us, or assassinated our character. The reality is that the struggle does not magically go away. The most tragic thing is sitting there and not doing anything about it.

I think the biggest question we have to ask ourselves is this: Do we really want to quit, or do we just want to throw in the towel? The saying goes: When you think about quitting, remember why you started. I have told those with whom I worked, those whom I have mentored and discipled and have the privilege to pastor, that if you throw in the towel, I will throw the towel right back at you. There's no quitting; there's no Plan B. There's only plan A, because it's God's perfect plan. Most of the time, when things go wrong, it's because we have a different plan from God's. We have a different theory, and we think for some reason that we know more than God knows. I heard a preacher once say, "If the shoe fits, wear it." In other words, if it's convicting to you, and if it's true, then accept it, but just know this: It doesn't define you.

I want to share with you a few things that have helped me get through this journey, because it's not easy. One thing I hold to is what the Bible says: "I can do all things through Christ who gives me strength," because it's not my strength and it's not my will, but it is His will. When I position myself to align with who God says I am, I'm able to gain the covering and the strength and the ability to move forward.

Do not merely listen to the word, and so deceive yourselves. Do what it says. Anyone who listens to the word but does not do what it says is like someone who looks at his face in a mirror and, after looking at himself, goes away and immediately forgets what he looks like. But whoever looks intently into the perfect law that gives freedom, and continues in it—not forgetting what they have heard, but doing it—they will be blessed in what they do. —James 1:22–25 NIV

I was in prayer one day when the Lord brought me to this Scripture, just like He has brought many of you. I've heard this Scripture mentioned many times. I've heard it preached in many different ways, but that day as I sat there, the Lord spoke to me: "Son, too many times people are being informed but they are not being transformed." In other words, we are gathering information. We're going to church, we're reading books, we're hearing online podcasts, and we're gaining information, but we're not doing anything with it, so we're not seeing any transformation taking place. For example, there is a statistic I came across, that if we hear something, we only retain up to about 10 percent of it, but if we hear it *and* we see it visually, the percentage goes up to 20 to 30 percent. But what really excited me was the other part I heard them say: If you *hear it* and you *see it* and you *do it*, the percentage goes up to 90 percent! We see a big difference from hearing it, but also not just hearing it but seeing it. The biggest breakthroughs are meant for those who follow through. A great mentor who is a Kingdom entrepreneur once said, "Breakthrough is meant for those who follow through and stay through; it's for the finishers."

We can't just be people who let the daily struggles and the conflicts around us keep us down.

For God did not give us a spirit of cowardice or fear, but [He has given us a spirit] of power and of love and of sound judgment and personal discipline [abilities that result in a calm, well-balanced mind and self-control]. —1 Timothy 1:7 AMP

Too many times people just sit there doing nothing because they've been informed but they haven't been transformed. The Bible says that faith without works is dead, so there is action we need to take on our end. The enemy's job is to divide and conquer. He wants to make us feel as if we're powerless, wondering how could ever God use someone like us. Truth be told, we will always be our own worst critic. We will judge ourselves more and hold ourselves to a higher degree, but something tells us that we're not worthy. We hear all of the lies that convince us we cannot overcome. God truly has restored us, and God has positioned us to take authority. It's time for you to take up the position that God has called you to walk in, because we are God's voice to a people, to a nation, to a community. We are called to bring hope—as the Bible says, a living hope—because we are the messengers who have resurrection power ready to be released. We can restore those who have been damaged and fragmented; we can heal those who are sick. We are called to expand God's Kingdom and take back territory from the enemy. We are to be the ambassadors that the Bible says we are. If we're just people who are just going to take in information and not do anything with it, we will never see or be the change that God intended us to be.

In closing, my pastor once said, "There are some things God will deliver you from, and there are some things you'll have to learn to discipline yourself through."

ABOUT J.D. JUAREZ

J.D Juarez is a husband, father, pastor & self-made Kingdom entrepreneur. Today I help people discover their WHO through applying biblical concepts & biblical principles to rediscovering their God given Identity & Purpose in life. I believe the bible is the best collections of profound wisdom & insights to apply for personal, family and business development.

10

TRUSTING

BY JASON CENTENO

Trust in the LORD with all thine heart, lean not unto thine own understanding. In all thy ways acknowledge him, and he shall direct thy paths.

—Proverbs 3:5–6 KJV

As I sit out here on the back porch of the Tampa home we moved into about ten months ago, I look over the small lake, trying to decide what I should write about, but nothing impressive comes to mind. And maybe that's what I'm supposed to be—unimpressive. How else is God supposed to shine through in my testimony, if I'm too busy trying to dazzle you with my rhetoric?

Some backstory first. I was presented with this opportunity by a friend and now business partner, Eric Skeldon. You may have read about him in another chapter of this book. And to be honest, I didn't really think I was worthy of this opportunity. I wouldn't call myself a "good Christian," whatever that means—

I guess we all define what that means differently. But I AM decidedly a Christ follower. Whenever I'm facing a tough moral dilemma, or even just the decisions that may cause me to pause, more times than not, I will try to think, *What would Jesus do?* I don't ask what the Church would do, or what my pastor, neighbor, father, or brother would do, but what would Jesus actually do?

I'm one of those Christians who grew up with church as a part of my household. I was a preacher's kid—or a "PK" for short. If you know anything about PKs, they are usually either "very Christian" or "very rebellious"—not many of them fall in between. I'm still not sure which category I would have fallen into, to be honest. I guess it would depend on who you asked!

My father was an "inner city youth," first-generation Puerto Rican kid whose parents didn't speak English, but they moved the family to Philadelphia for better opportunities. My father succumbed to the influence of the streets at an early age. He was actually a member of a gang before he was even a teenager. His lack of purpose and despair eventually grew so great that he decided the world would be better off without him. He planned to commit suicide. One weekend, however, he was offered the opportunity to go to a Christian camp retreat, and he thought that would be a good place to do what he intended to do. At least he would spare his family the horror of finding his body. But as it happened, God had a different plan for him, and during that weekend at Teen Haven, he came to know Christ.

I bring up this portion of my family history only because if it wasn't for that sequence of events, it's pretty obvious you wouldn't be reading these words, as I wouldn't exist. And also quite frankly, I want to reaffirm to myself that God has a purpose for me...even though I don't quite know what His ultimate purpose is just yet. I also have the feeling that someone who may be reading this right now is feeling the exact same way. His purpose hasn't been revealed for you yet, and maybe that has really discouraged you lately. I want to speak more than anything to that one person and tell you that, until He calls you home, God isn't finished with you yet.

Like my father before me, I grew up in the inner city of Philadelphia, because that is where my father's heart and ministry was. He wanted to impact the lives of those who were lost, just like he once was, and he did a pretty good job of it, too. My dad is kind of a legend inside the Hispanic community for his work within the community and on the streets of Philadelphia, as a missionary, a pastor, and more recently a police department chaplain. Pastor Luis Centeno, go look him up.

I grew up in a Christian household surrounded by the streets, and I was one of those kids who developed both book smarts and street smarts. Even to this day, I couldn't tell you how my parents managed it financially, but they definitely sacrificed a lot for me to have a private Christian school education. I thank God for that, because even though I can't say I was fully invested in it at the time, my upbringing laid the groundwork and planted the seeds in me for me, later in life, to eventually return back to the fold. But as I like to say sometimes, I guess I needed to wander around for forty years in the desert before I could develop a deeper relationship with Christ. I'm not saying that my lifestyle until my forties was particularly bad; I'm just saying that I don't feel like I was living for anything in particular other than myself, if I'm being honest.

I did all the things you're supposed to do: graduate from college, get a real job, start a family. I finally settled into a career as a firefighter, and I would spend twenty-three years of my life working for the city of Philadelphia. During my time working as a Philadelphia firefighter, I finally also developed into an entrepreneur. I began investing in real estate and got into some other business opportunities, as well: some that panned out, many more that didn't. It was also during that time that my life began to take a much wilder ride, one I didn't really notice I was stuck on until it was almost too late.

Success and money can turn things funny in life, especially when you are under a lot of stress. I would say that's what led to my dark period, although at the time, it seemed quite the opposite. For many years, I was just a regular firefighter, a "ladder" or a "truck" guy, if you know the job. But in 2004, a deputy chief offered me a more specialized position within the fire department due to my background in digital filmmaking. I accepted it, and I became one of the "Four Horsemen of the Apocalypse": a member of the visual communications unit. We did a lot of things, but most notably, have you ever seen that show *CSI*, where they conduct forensic investigations, and there's the main detective and then the guys taking the pictures of the scenes behind them who get no dialogue? Well, the fire department's version of that was a fire marshal who will lead the investigation and a VCU member who would gather and curate the photographic evidence of the victims. That's right, I took pictures of dead bodies and disasters for a living. I was one of only four guys in the whole department who had that onerous honor. What I didn't realize was all the damaging psychological effects that seeing so much death, that often and so up close and personal, I was experiencing, to the point that I developed post-traumatic stress disorder—PTSD—although that wasn't professionally identified until years later, when it resurfaced toward the end of my firefighting career.

My time in VCU certainly added to the dark depths of my decadence. As I understand it, when you have PTSD, you can either retreat deeply into yourself and self-medicate, or you can alternatively grow aggressive and violent, or maybe just act out more. In my case, I acted out more, becoming a party boy, experiencing everything in excess. Every day my motto was "live for today, for tomorrow isn't promised," except I took that idea to negative, selfish extremes. The best way I can describe it is that when I saw the dead bodies of a young mother cradling her four children, or a mother who in despair had murdered her own son, then committed suicide, it felt like more and more dirt was piling into my soul, and I would do ANYTHING to wash that feeling away. And that's what I did, mostly off-duty, but to be honest, occasionally even while still on duty. Although I thought I hid it well, eventually my behavior began to threaten my marriage, my relationships with those around me, and even my job, when I was confronted about my attitude and actions. I thank God that He surrounded me with good people because eventually I was able to, with some effort and help, turn things around and start my journey back toward a personal relationship with God.

All this happened for a reason.

During that time, my wife and I had a son. We tried to have other children, but after many attempts, doctor evaluations, and painful procedures, we were still unable to conceive again. God laid it upon our hearts to explore adoption. It wasn't our original intention. In the beginning, it wasn't any more than us just wishing to have a little girl and then that would be it. But that one step set us on a journey that neither of us ever imagined for ourselves, because if we had, we might have said, "Thanks for the offer but we'll pass."

We currently have six children total, and five of them are adopted. That wasn't our intention (did I mention that yet?), but that is the path God laid out for us. He sent us a few guides to help along the way. It started with some friends. We started going back to church, choosing one named Bethel where we already knew a few of the members. One of the pastors there, Chris Hanley, along with his wife, Kelli, had adopted six children, and these two people later became some of our dearest friends. They helped guide us along in the adoption process.

God began to reveal Himself to me in amazing ways during this process. In fact, because I can be pretty dense sometimes, He even went so far as to "tap me on the shoulder" one day to get my attention and let me know this was His purpose for my life. I'll explain.

By this time, we had already adopted Kaleb successfully, and soon after, we found ourselves fostering to adopt a little girl, as we had planned for from the beginning. In my mind, we were all set now—we had three children, along with a three-bedroom house in a nice neighborhood, and we were comfortable. I was done—mission accomplished. But the case workers kept sending us more children to consider. My wife would ask me about them, but I would say no. I wanted to focus on the kids we already had. I had no desire for any more children, because to be honest, more meant we would need a bigger house, bigger cars, bigger bills, and I didn't want any of that. Selfish? Maybe. But hey, men are built to be logical, and that's what I was being.

One Sunday during the service, Pastor Rob Tarnovesky gave a sermon about that one person out there who really needed our help—and how God would show each of us who that was. We didn't have to concern ourselves with evangelizing to the masses or even doing great work, God was trying alert us to the one person out there who needed our help now. We were not to be so blinded by our own hopes and dreams that we missed that one person who needed us the most. We needed to just look. That "ONE PERSON"—that phrase kept hammering me over and over in my head. Of course, Pastor Rob had no idea that in the previous week the agency had contacted us multiple times regarding a four-year-old boy they were having difficulty placing because of his unique set of circumstances. He was currently living in a household where they only spoke Spanish, and the caseworkers couldn't find any other qualified foster parents available. So there was this little blond-haired, blue-eyed boy with whom nobody could communicate and they didn't know what to do with him, so they kept reaching out to us. Every time they asked, I told my wife "no."

Although my mind had already been made up, when the pastor kept repeating the words "one person," I couldn't take it anymore. I groaned so loudly that people turned around and looked at us. My wife elbowed me, as if to say, "What's wrong with you?" I replied, "Are you hearing this?" She looked back at the pastor, nodded slightly, and said, "I think so." And that was it. God has never been more clear to me than He was in that moment. I sighed and just surrendered. "I guess we should call the caseworker tomorrow and go get him."

That day stands out to me as the day when my mission was revealed. It was to eventually become my "big why," my purpose, that I was meant to be instrumental in the adoption of one hundred children into their forever homes before I die. I want that to be my legacy. Now, that didn't become fully clear to me all at once—that didn't happen until I saw the video. There is a Facebook video that still circulates today about Nicholas Winton, a gentleman who was recognized for his part in saving more than six hundred children from the Nazis during World War II. At one point, the host asked, "Is there anyone in our audience tonight who owes their life to Nicholas Winton? If so, could you stand up please?" The *entire* audience stood up—they were all the kids he had saved! Mr. Winton stood to survey the crowd, taking it in, then he returned to his seat, wiping the tears from his eyes. No more words were needed. When I saw this video, I said to myself, "That. I want that." So from that moment in church, that "tap on the shoulder from God," followed by seeing that specific video, that is where my mission in life became clear. It is to make sure that one hundred children are adopted into forever homes through my influence and actions before I die. So now, as I journey through life, everything I do is directed toward that "why." I just need to save more kids.

I don't feel like I've been called to move crowds or speak over nations or anything on a grander scale. That sort of prestige doesn't really excite me. I always go back to that moment in church where I heard the words, "Help just one person." Okay, I can handle that. Who? Then I go back to that Nicholas Winton video. Save kids. Copy that. I have my orders. I'm here to facilitate the adoption of more children into their forever homes, one child at a time, one family at a time, as many times as I can. That's the mission. Everything else is secondary.

What does that look like for me right now? What are my daily or weekly activities? Right now, it just involves having a lot of conversations. Since 2014, I began making it a habit to bring up my intention to see one hundred children adopted into forever homes before I die, which I refer to as "my #journeyto100" now, in any conversation I can slide it into. Not in an obnoxious way, like a vegan who brings veganism up over even the most trifling of excuses! But if the conversation turns into "so, what do you do?" then usually I will find an opportunity to share my mission, because I think you should always share why you do what you do with others you encounter. It's a way to connect to them on a deeper level in a world where everything is so surface-oriented. I've lost count of how many people I've met who were fostered or adopted or interested in adopting folks. I've built deeper relationships with them just through that, and there are some I've been able to counsel as they become more interested. I'm officially retired now, but I still consult regularly with people who were referred to me or who seek me out regarding entrepreneurship, real estate investing, and tech-related business ventures. And I have my #journeyto100 conversation with almost everyone who comes my way. I let them know that this is my "why." Anything I do for you, whether it's helping your business increase its cash flow, helping you realize your dream and develop an app that will change the world, or anything else you ask of me, I'm willing to say, "Okay, and here's the deal. I've told you about my mission, so if I'm able to help you in whatever way you are asking me to, and as a result of my help you become financially blessed and successful, and you can agree that yes, I helped get you to that point, all I ask of you is that you remember what I shared with you about my mission, and if there is room in your heart and home for one more, that you would seriously consider adoption and then reach out to me and ask me about how to go about it."

Of course, I practice what I preach. Since starting this mission, my wife and I have adopted five of our own children, and we have contributed our support in the adoption of three others. So, by my count, we have at least ninety-two more kids to go. But I believe that it's going to happen, some way, somehow. Maybe even one of them will be adopted by you reading this book. Hint, hint.

I'm not exactly a great Christian. In fact, I feel I should be wearing a T-shirt that says, "I love Jesus but I cuss a little." I'm just a retired firefighter who happened to get lucky, trying to take whatever odd talents and gifts God has given me and use them for the greater good while I still have time on this third rock from the sun. So, I use my time to help build up Dad Entrepreneurs so they can become better dads, which helps me to get better myself. I now also spend more time helping Kingdom business owners, for the same reason. I will find one hundred ways to help one hundred dads become better dads, better men, and successful family men, because, well, they seem the likeliest to consider joining me along my "Journey to 100" to see one hundred and more kids adopted into forever homes. One hundred millionaire dads could adopt one hundred kids! What a headline that would make!

This path I'm on, I can't see all of it. I just see the mountaintop. And my eyes are fixed on that. I will stumble. There will be forks in the road. I may take a wrong turn and have to turn back, retrace my steps, and go a different way. I can say for certain there will be failures—lots of them. But my heart tells me, "This is the way."

At the beginning of this chapter, I shared Proverbs 3:5–6 (KJV): "Trust in the LORD with all thine heart, lean not unto thine own understanding. In all thy ways acknowledge him, and he shall direct thy paths." If you're reading this book, you're most likely looking for words of inspiration from Kingdom authors, Kingdom-centered people. But what could I say that could possibly top this verse?

I'll leave you with this. If you're out there struggling, looking for meaning, unsure of your purpose or your path, just trust in Him. God will find you. God will help you along the way. Don't worry about how long it takes. If you trust Him, and just begin to acknowledge Him in all your ways, He will direct your path, just as He directs mine. The evidence is there—it's all around you.

There's this thing my dad likes to say. Whenever anybody asks my dad how he's doing, he always responds by saying, "Trusting," which means he's always trusting in God's promises. And that's kind of beautiful, isn't it? Anyway, I thought that was cool because that's what I'm doing now. I'm "trusting."

I believe God's purpose for me in this chapter was to communicate His message to you. If you feel like you haven't found your purpose yet, if you're still feeling a little lost and maybe you just need to have a more personal conversation with a fellow sojourner to give you some validation that you're on God's chosen path, I hope to be that person for you. For anyone reading who still might not know their purpose, if we were this very moment traveling together, shoulder to shoulder, a little out of breath from our recent climb out of a valley, headed toward our promised land, I would say to you, "How are you doing?" And like my father says, you would smile and reply, "Ah, I'm trusting." And then we would probably do a fist-bump, because that's what travel buddies do.

See you on the road. Keep on trusting.

ABOUT JASON CENTENO

Jason Centeno is a retired Philadelphia Firefighter and tech-savvy entrepreneur Jason Centeno founded Trashmitter in 2021 to specifically combat the enormous waste, litter, and filth problems that have been plaguing metropolitan areas like his hometown of Philadelphia. Trashmitter functions like an "Uber for Trash" providing homeowners and small businesses with an easy button to deal with trash emergencies quickly so they can get back to doing what matters most: protecting their investments and enjoying their lives.

To date Trashmitter has been successfully running a pre-pilot program in Philadelphia since October 2021. It is on track to officially launch its pilot program in Philadelphia in Q2 2022, and then expand nationwide by the end of 2022.

In addition Jason has always had passion for entrepreneurship and helping others develop their big ideas into tech companies. Some of his most notable contributions include the Workbnb app, the US Housing Exchange app, and the Kingdom Warrior NFT Project.

Jason currently resides with his wife Luz and 6 children in Tampa Florida and spends most of his downtime wrangling his 6 children, crafting immaculate Dad jokes, and teasing the gators in the lake out back of his house.

https://www.instagram.com/thedadnextdoor_/

jasoncanfixanything@gmail.com

11

LIVING PEACE

BY MICHAEL WADLOW

> You will keep in perfect peace
> those whose minds are steadfast,
> because they trust in you.
> —Isaiah 26:3 NIV

Wait! They sold the house?! They never even told us they were sending it to auction?!

Unbeknownst to me, I was beginning the long process of learning to stand on the promises and faithfulness of God, producing a faith that would lead to rest.

The house sold Monday morning at the courthouse for $180,000 cash to an investment group, $100,000 less than what we had offered. This was after nine long months of proving our income to the bank, waiting, and praying.

Back in 2003, while we were living in a rental house, the Lord gave my wife, Amy, and I the verse, Deuteronomy 8:18, which I took to be a promise that He meant to prosper us, and not just financially: "But you shall remember the LORD your God, for it is He who is giving you power to make wealth, that He may confirm His covenant which He swore to your fathers..." (NASB). This was a covenant that was given in the context of the Israelites entering the Promised Land.

We were looking to move out of our first home. We needed a larger garage for the equipment I would use in my new business endeavor. We were in the middle of the economic recession of 2008, and my friend was selling this home as a short sale. I, too, had taken a big hit to my income as an electrical contractor.

We had asked the Lord to close the door if it wasn't the right house for us, but when it was sent to auction, the situation was still painful. It felt like an injustice the way it had occurred. "Okay, Lord," Amy prayed, "if this is not Your best for us, I release it. Show us what You have for us instead." That evening, she found a farmhouse on a couple acres, that backed up to over 1,400 acres of cattle land, and it also had a shop. She was excited to show me the listing.

I had wanted a home with land and a view, but I was certain this was not it. It was a beautiful property, with mature trees, solar panels, and a shop. It was a large house with spacious views, but it needed a ton of work! Even my dad said, "I would hate to see you buy this. You will never be done with it." However, when we went to take a second look, I walked right into a divine change of heart. In a single moment, the Lord shifted my perspective, and we made an offer on the farmhouse.

Just before escrow closed on our new house, God made reference to His "8:18 promise." I went by to talk to the owner, and he showed me around, telling me about the grapes, pomegranates, and figs growing on the property. When I left, he sent me off with two huge clusters of grapes. I couldn't help but think of the men sent to spy out the Promised Land in the Old Testament.

When I got home, I read the story of the twelve men who were sent to spy out the land of Canaan. They had cut down a huge cluster of grapes and carried it between two men, and they also brought back some of the pomegranates and the figs. I was excited. What was God doing? I wondered.

We got the keys to the house on September 11, 2009. We had intended to fix up the house one room at a time, but before long, we had really torn it up, living from paycheck to paycheck as we remodeled. At one point, we only had a sink in the laundry area, a single working toilet in the downstairs bathroom, and only a shower in the upstairs bathroom. There was a hole in the floor where the kitchen used to be, and we cooked on an electric burner sitting on a half sheet of plywood resting on sawhorses in the middle of the room. Up to that point, I had never felt so overwhelmed.

One evening after work, I looked at our shell of a house and said out loud, "I can't do it, Lord. It's too much. We don't have enough money, and this is too much work for me." Almost immediately, I heard Him respond in my heart, *I have given you what you need to finish what you can work on right now. I will supply for the next thing when you are ready to work on it.*

In that season, we learned a number of things as we remodeled that house with the Lord. We learned that where He leads, He supplies, and that resources flow where there is faith, leading to expectant preparation and planning. As we neared the completion of each task and planned for the next, the needed provision came. Sometimes it was more income from work;

sometimes it was volunteer labor from friends; and sometimes it was God's miraculous supply.

Right after I finished remodeling the laundry room, I met a man whom the Lord had already prompted to bless us, a man who owned a cabinet shop. He built our kitchen cabinets for us, just as we had designed them, including paying his crew to install them, for free.

We also learned that God honors discipline and self-control. We disciplined ourselves in our spending, making tithing a priority. During that time, there were moments when God would multiply our finances. Amy would say, "We shouldn't have this much money." One night we were looking at the bills that were due, but we lacked the money. We began to pray, and in a moment of clarity, I began to chuckle. After all we had learned and all we had seen God do, it was absurd to think that our Father would not provide for us now. I started laughing. I couldn't even make a request. All I could do was praise Him and thank Him in advance. The provision came the next day!

Phase one of our remodel was the downstairs. We learned to rely on the Lord in a way that led us from anxious prayers to often giving thanks in advance. We were growing in our faith and understanding, and He was giving us peace and rest.

It took about seven years of hard work, in addition to our regular jobs and on top of the ministry we were doing. There were lots of trials—let's just say Chip and Joanna have nothing on us. Things frequently didn't go the way we planned. We learned to fight in order to see God above the circumstances, to strengthen ourselves through praise. We would declare the promises and character of God in the face of the hardest moments, for as long as it would take, until His peace and presence overshadowed us, and frustration, hopelessness, and anxiety left.

Psalm 91:2 models this prayer for us: "I will say to the LORD, 'My refuge and my fortress, my God, in whom I trust'" (NASB). I would literally take my attention off of the problem and exalt the reality of God in praise, giving fear and the circumstances no room to capture my gaze.

The circumstances were the facts, but God is Truth. Repeatedly, we found that clinging to the truth about Him led to Him changing the facts. As many have said, "What you focus on, you empower."

In the first few years at our new home, we decided it was time to have children, but that didn't happen for a while. It took seven or eight years of praying and trying, and even consulting some doctors, only to find out there was no obvious reason we couldn't conceive. During that time, friends and family were praying for us regularly. I responded to altar calls for those wanting to get pregnant, even if Amy wasn't there. I, especially, was very anxious at times.

The circumstances seemed to be saying that we might not have a child of our own, and a few well-meaning people even told us, "Maybe it's not God's will for you to have children." However, I didn't want to listen to circumstances or the opinions of man.

Instead, I spent time meditating on verses about children being a blessing from the Lord, and God's promise to Israel in Deuteronomy 7, that there would be no barrenness or miscarriages. Even though the context of Deuteronomy is a covenant with Israel that did not directly pertain to me, I began to see God's heart for His people. I began to pray, asking Him for a child with new faith. It was painful at times, but we learned to rest in the Lord. Our faith was not in our desired outcome. Our faith was in our good and faithful God. He would meet us in this, just as He had in everything else. (This is not meant to be a commentary on anyone else's journey; it is just our personal story.)

Finally, after many years, the Lord supplied a unique solution. A friend told us about an acupuncturist who had helped her to get pregnant. Amy visited this acupuncturist twice, and in less than thirty days, she was pregnant. Long before having children, we had determined to name our son Kaenan, if we had a boy, because of the promise from Deuteronomy 8:18. This would be our declaration that we believed and trusted in Him.

During Amy's pregnancy with Kaenan, we decided to remodel the upstairs. After some counsel, it was determined that the best course of action would be to completely remove the roof and second floor and start over. This led to another season of trials, which taught us to stand on the Word of God and trust His ways. "Garments of praise for the spirit of heaviness" became our lifestyle out of necessity (see Isaiah 61:3), because it was so hard at first, but we watched miracle after miracle take place as we chose to look to, and exalt, the Lord.

When Amy was about eight months' pregnant, one of our friends came over to take some pregnancy pictures of her. It was late fall, and the skies were dark with clouds. As soon as we started taking pictures, a strong storm suddenly blew in, and the rain began to pour down. The wind ripped huge tarps from our unfinished roof, and water began streaming into our house; through our new second-floor insulation, into the first-floor ceilings, through the light fixtures, and onto our furniture and newly remodeled carpets and hardwood floors downstairs.

Amy sat down and cried, understandably, but the Lord gave grace. I began to worship, which was surprisingly easy, and do what I could to encourage Amy and save the floors. The day after the storm, a contractor friend offered us twelve floor fans, for free, which saved our floors.

We spent a lot of money and time on our remodel. We never stopped seeking the Kingdom of God, but at times I really struggled with condemnation. The enemy would attack me when I was tired and run down with religious performance and a poverty mind-set. I would feel guilty for our vision of a beautiful home and nice things. Interestingly, when my eyes were on the Lord, I never once felt that way, and often I felt quite the opposite.

By wisdom a house is built, and by understanding it is established; and by knowledge the rooms are filled with all precious and pleasant riches.—Proverbs 24:3–4 NASB

Another of the enemy's strategies was to remind me that years before, God had called me to some kind of ministry. I had tried figure out what and how He wanted me to do, but there was never a clear vision or path. I was currently leading a small ministry school, but I knew there was more to it. I began struggling emotionally as an electrical contractor, because I had lost the heart for it, but we needed the money for the remodel. There was a real temptation to resent our home at times. I had to keep declaring the goodness and faithfulness of God, laboring to entering His rest. I had to strengthen myself in the Lord.

In the summer of 2018, Amy and I agreed to take a leap of faith. I left the electrical trade to pursue the Lord concerning the ministry He had called me to; we were sacrificing my income. I didn't know what was next or how to get there, but we were in agreement and we had peace.

Then, on November 8, 2018, we saw the hand of God that had gone before us. I had called for the final inspection on our four-bedroom, almost completely rebuilt farmhouse. As I headed to the store before the inspector arrived, I saw thick, dark smoke filling the skies from up the hill near Paradise, California. My parents, my dad's parents, and my mom's mom all lived up there. That day, as the inspector looked over all our hard work, after years of literal blood, sweat, and tears, a tight budget, disaster after disaster, and regularly fighting to enter God's rest, my entire family all moved into our beautiful, peacefully finished home. All of our loved ones had lost everything in the Camp Fire.

My grandfather died two months later. My family handled it all very well, trusting the Lord and walking together. They were all so thankful for a warm, peaceful place to take care of all their insurance paperwork, and to grieve, rest, and be together through such a difficult and traumatic time. Repeatedly, they spoke of the peace they had while staying in our home. It was clear to all of us that God had gone before us, preparing a place of rest for each member of my family. I can't help but think of Jesus saying that He left this world to go and prepare a place for us to be with Him, where He is.

As for the leap of faith, my family's insurance policies paid us rent while they lived with us. Amy later pointed out to me, "After all the time you spent trying to figure it out, when you let go, He provided." This income allowed me to continue to train in our ministry school, and now also online.

If I could give anyone a single piece of advice, it would be to become an expert in praise. This is, in one sense, meditating on Him. If you will learn to exalt Him and His promises in the hardest of times, actively abiding in Him for as long as it takes to believe or to break through, you will be met by God in amazing ways. Rather than trials weighing you down, they will become opportunities to see His glory be manifested in your life.

A couple more things that we learned along the way:

"Those who have will be given more." This Kingdom principle, along with growing in discipline, opens up supernatural results. Mind-sets change, and provision flows. See Matthew 13:12; 25:29.

When His presence comes, His Kingdom will come, His provision will flow, and there will be peace, rest, and prosperity. But this is only a taste of the fullness yet to be realized. "God himself is at rest. And at the end of the journey we'll surely rest with God. So let's keep at it and eventually arrive at the place of rest..." (Hebrews 4:10–11 MSG).

"[May] our God make you worthy of his calling, and that by his power he may bring to fruition your every desire for goodness and your every deed prompted by faith" (2 Thessalonians 1:11 NIVUK).

ABOUT MICHAEL WADLOW

Michael learned to walk with the Holy Spirit during his 20 plus years in construction. Through prayer, prophecy, the gospel and the working of miracles, he saw lives impacted by the kingdom. He is now encouraging and equipping kingdom ambassadors and revivalists to walk in their Biblical and prophetic identity and to reveal the kingdom of God in love and power. Michael, his wife Amy and son Kaenan live in Chico, California where he leads Empowered Ministry School, trains in prophecy and supernatural living online. Passionate about the image of God and His kingdom, Michael has a strong conviction that the world should see the Father when they see his people.

Michael is also the author of They Will Have Visions, a handbook for growing people in the experience of visions and other communication by the Holy Spirit.

https://www.instagram.com/michaeldavid41

My Book

12

UPGRADE YOUR MINDSET

BY DAVID B. & KATIE MARIE HUGHES

"Set your minds on things above, not on earthly things."
—Colossians 3:2 NIV

No matter who you are or what your life is like currently, God has a much greater realm of living available for you to move into. Jesus said in John 10:10, "I have come to give you everything in abundance, more than you expect—life in its fullness until you overflow!" (The Passion Translation)

In order for this to happen, we must exchange our lower level thoughts for higher level thoughts. Higher thinking leads to higher living. This higher life is one of greater purpose, fulfillment, and impact.

I grew up in an amazing family with great parents and siblings who loved the Lord. I was taught how to trust and follow Him in a true personal relationship, which helped form the foundation of my faith in Jesus Christ. I am forever deeply grateful for that. Even though my dad and mom loved the Lord, many years of their marriage were filled with stress and struggle in the area of finances. This was due to my dad's depression and decisions that led to him not working for years at a time. Experiencing those dynamics growing up, I remember making a decision in my childhood that I never wanted to be in that position financially with my future wife and family. I knew I wanted to live on the other side of money, where money would be working for me rather than me working for it. I decided I would do my part of seeking out the people who had adopted this way of life, and I would be completely teachable to follow their instructions in order to live life full time with no limitations, pursuing all of the God-given dreams in my heart. That's what I did, and that's what happened. The greatest success book of all time, the Bible, is clear that we should seek wisdom and instruction from those who have it and then follow the instructions with a teachable heart.

Jesus lived an overflow life as well. Just look at the examples: Shortly after Jesus' birth it said in Matthew 2:11 (NIV) "Then they opened their treasures and presented him with gifts of gold, frankincense and myrrh." One moment with Jesus, the disciples had an abundant catch of fish! Another moment describes Jesus multiplying five loaves of bread and two fish, to feed thousands! We also hear of a wealthy woman funding Jesus' ministry in Luke 8. It doesn't take long reading through the gospels to see that Jesus lived His life in the overflow.

Cashflow is not the answer, cash-OVER-flow is the answer to living a life of financial freedom and abundance. With financial freedom and abundance flowing into and through your life, you can live out your dreams, passions, and purposes maximally.

In Genesis 1:28, God said to His creation of male and female, ""Prosper! Reproduce! Fill Earth! Take charge!" (The Message)

In order to carry out our ultimate mission and assignment God gave us here, we must learn how to steward and utilize the resources He made available to us in the best ways.

Today, my wife and I have rushing rivers of revenue perpetually flowing and growing into our life while we are sleeping, laying on the beach with each other, and pursuing all the dreams in our hearts with no limitations. This is available to everyone. It's much easier to do than many of the things you have done already in your life, like learning how to walk, learning the English language, raising children, etc. etc. I have learned that living the truly abundant life in all areas is simple. To me, it can be summed up in one word...POSITIONING. The positioning (or alignment) of our mind (thoughts), heart, and life with God's Word and His Ways is what produces perpetual multiplication of abundance in all areas of our lives. So, if it's really that simple, why are most people living a life of far less than their God-given dreams and potential? It is because most people are lying to themselves without even realizing it. They agree with lies, which is reflected in the life of limitations they live.

Learning to think higher thoughts, leads to living a higher life. He said, "My thoughts are higher than your thoughts." He is always inviting us into a higher realm of thinking, with new perspectives, insights, and strategies. The only question is...Are you willing to go there? Because in order to go there, it requires letting go of your current ways of thinking and perceiving. It requires letting go of what others might think or say about you. It requires letting go of leaning on your own understanding. It requires letting go of your comfort zones. In order to receive new wine, you must have new wine skin. Therefore, in order to receive new realms of abundant blessings, you must discard the old ways of thinking and take on a new mindset.

The Bible is a love story about a Father, His Son, The King, and His Kingdom in which He invites each one of us into experiencing success and abundance with Him, far beyond what we've ever known or imagined. My wife and I currently specialize in showing people how to position themselves properly to live a life of financial overflow so they can live out their God-given dreams to the maximum!

It says in 2 Chronicles 20:20 "Have faith in the Lord your God and you will be upheld; have faith in his prophets and you will be successful." It is very interesting to me that it's chapter 20 and verse 20, like 20/20 vision. This reminds me that people help bring perfect clarity and execution to your vision. These prophets and mentors help to propel you into the fullness of your Kingdom purpose.

"You will find true success when you find me, for I have insight into wise plans that are designed just for you." -Proverbs 8:14 TPT

"Wise instruction is like a costly gem. It turns the impossible into success." -Proverbs 17:8 TPT

"Keep this Book of the Law always on your lips; meditate on it day and night, so that you may be careful to do everything written in it. Then you will be prosperous and successful." -Joshua 1:8 NIV

"In everything he did he had great success, because the Lord was with him."

-I Samuel 18:14 NIV

"As long as he sought the Lord, God gave him success." -II Chronicles 26:5 NIV

"If the ax is dull and its edge unsharpened, more strength is needed, but skill will bring success." -Ecclesiastes 10:10 NIV

Jesus shows us how to sharpen our mind (the ax) with His Word which leads to abundant success.

Jesus said, "According to your faith, let it be done to you." -Matthew 9:29 NIV

"And Jesus grew in wisdom and stature, and in favor with God and man." -Luke 2:52

-David B. Hughes

Throughout my life, I've observed that most people are looking for a magic bullet, secret answer, or a quick fix in life. Just about everyone wants to know "The simple 5 steps to..." without really getting back to basics and pondering the wisdom they have already been given.

Truth be told, the answer to just about every question in life begins with MINDSET. Breaking this word down, we can easily see the most important step of all ... SET your MIND. If our lives aren't flowing out of proper perspective in every area, we will be unsuited and misaligned with the goals we so desperately long to achieve. We can desire to have a Kingdom Mind all day everyday, but if we haven't set our minds properly, we will just be wishing and hoping, running around on the same hamster wheel of frustration and lack of results.

God has placed huge, audacious dreams inside each and every one of us and no two dreamers' dreams are the same. However, in order to accomplish and flourish in the fruition of those dreams, we must get back to basics.

And so, I ask you just one question: what is it that God last asked you to do that you have not yet done? Ouch. That question even stings a bit as I type it. You are not alone in your unfinished to-do's and, "I'll get to it someday's" of life. We have all been there and most of us are still there in some area or another.

After all, it's much easier to get excited at the beginning of a project or task than to see it through to completion. But I believe this completion is the key to God opening up greater realms and dimensions in our lives.

If we can't be trusted to follow through on the last instruction we received from the One who made us, what makes us think we can successfully move forward into bigger things?

May this truth be a catapulting encouragement to you, as it is to me. Let us stop for just a few moments in our hectic lives to ponder the things we have left undone. Then, let's take one baby step at a time towards accomplishing these things.

As we become good stewards of the tasks and dreams God has already called us to, He will begin to open up dimensions of thriving in every area of our lives and help us bring others along on this exciting journey of obedience. Now, let's get to it ... the world is waiting for your unique brilliance!

"The one who faithfully manages the little he has been given will be promoted and trusted with greater responsibilities. But those who cheat with the little they have been given will not be considered trustworthy to receive more." - Luke 16:10 TPT

We have learned unique and powerful strategies that can catapult anyone from where they are to where they dream to be and beyond. We love helping people get unlocked and unleashed into the limitless lives they were designed and destined to live in all areas!

-Katie Marie Hughes

DAVID B. & KATIE MARIE HUGHES

David B Hughes is passionate about living a maximized life and empowering others to do the same! He is an author, speaker, entrepreneur, business owner, investor, business coach, licensed realtor, and real estate investing coach. He has created multiple successful companies and has helped many others find, follow, and fulfill their God-given dreams and purposes.

Katie Marie Hughes' life is one of relentless passion and pursuit. She became a professional dancer at the age of 17. At the age of 22, she and her brother formed a nationally distributed Christian pop group, 3.16. She has shared stages with some of the top names in Christian music and has appeared in radio, television, magazines, and countless live venues. As a singer, songwriter, musician, dancer, author, worship pastor, speaker, and entrepreneur, Katie Marie lives to inspire others to reach their greatest potential.

David and Katie are the founders of LOVEco and Simplified Investing

https://www.instagram.com/davidbhughes55

https://www.instagram.com/lifewithkatiemarie

CONCLUSION

To accomplish great things, we must not only act, but also dream; not only plan, but also believe. -Anatole France

So what now? You have heard all these wonderful stories and seen the mysteries of how the Kingdom operates. You may be feeling like wow, but how does this apply to me? How do I enter into this wonderful Kingdom family? You simply ask and believe and step into your divine dance with the Creator of the Cosmos and Jesus. Matthew 6:33 (ESV) says, But seek first the kingdom of God and his righteousness, and all these things will be added to you.

I challenge you to declare and seek The Kingdom and God mysteries with Holy Spirit the rest of your life. It won't always be easy sometimes it's downright uncomfortable. The renewing of your mind and revelation of resting in God and the finished work can be one of the toughest things for believers. I believe because Western Culture tells us to always be going, consuming, doing, but we are Human BEING's not Human Doing's.

We must learn to access the easy yoke Jesus paid for to step into the heavenly mindset and perspective that is available to us. It's as easy as a baby sleeping and knowing their Papa and Mom love them.

We must go back to when we were kids. Before the first words of limitations were spoken over us. Loose them from our soul and find a place that does heart healing. Forgive your Fathers and Mothers and anyone who has wronged you. Jesus paid for that too. Become childlike again where we believe we can fly and live in love.

Matthew 18:3 ESV And said, "Truly, I say to you, unless you turn and become like children, you will never enter the kingdom of heaven.

I also encourage you as you develop the habit of renewing your mind and transforming your thoughts into your divine rights walking with Jesus that you speak them out loud. God created the Heavens and Earth with the words out of His mouth. Our words carry life and death so watch what you speak over you or another of God's creation. The book of James is great for all things taming the tongue. Speaking the bible out loud and also meditation and walking with God morning and night has been one of the most transforming things in my kingdom journey. The more honey on my lips the more revelation of His love for me and the more I crave his water well that never runs dry.

If you have made it this far you are a finisher and I give you the finishers anointing to have the power to finish whatever God plans for you to accomplish in your day. Habakkuk 2:2 And the LORD answered me: "Write the vision; make it plain on tablets, so he may run who reads it. So I encourage you to also start writing down the revelation you receive from God and prophetic words given over your life. Writing stuff down and speaking them out loud lets your brain retain information allowing transformation to accelerate. I am honored that you read this and am excited for your journey. I have made a place for Kingdom Citizens a free Facebook group. If you would like an invite and be encouraged and some weekly coaching and kingdom community join here <u>www.TheKingdomMind/Community</u>

I leave you with this scripture a mentor left me with before going transitioning to Heaven, after completing His race.

Numbers 6:24-26 The Lord bless you and keep you; the Lord make his face to shine upon you and be gracious to you; the Lord lift up his countenance upon you and give you peace.

~Eric

ABOUT KINGDOM WARRIORS NFT LORE

ILEYDRIA: THE GENESIS - 1

THE WAR'S BEEN RAGING FOR YEARS AROUND US; TWO EMPIRES LOCKED INTO A BATTLE THAT TOUCHED EVERY FACET OF OUR LAND. NOW, ILEYDRIA LIVES UNDER THE UMBRELLA OF THIS FIGHT, WONDERING... WAITING... WHO WILL BE VICTORIOUS?

IN A LIFETIME LONG FORGOTTEN, ILEYDRIA WAS FILLED WITH BOUNTY. OUR FIRES ROARED STRONG IN WINTER AND IN SUMMER, WE WERE MERRY. THE EVERLIGHT, HAVING SELECTED A MORTAL KING, REIGNED THROUGH HIM AND MANY WERE CONTENT.

WITHIN THE EVERLIGHT, MERE MEN BECAME GIANTS; PRACTICING HONOR, INTEGRITY, AND TRUTH. KINGDOM WARRIORS GREW IN DEVOTION TO THE EVERLIGHT, RECEIVING GIFTS OF WISDOM, PEACE, AND POWER. ALL WONDERED, WHAT COULD OVERWHELM SUCH A PLACE - WHERE LOVE, LIFE, AND CLARITY ROLLED ACROSS THE LAND LIKE THE COMING OF A SUMMER STORM?

AND YET... THE WELLS OF GOOD FORTUNE WERE POISONED. SLOWLY, THE WORLD FELT IT. SOMETHING DARK CREPT IN THE NIGHT. SOMETHING SINISTER AND VICIOUS, SOMETHING WITH GNASHING TEETH AND A WILY MIND. THE OBSIDIAN SHADE WAS BORN.

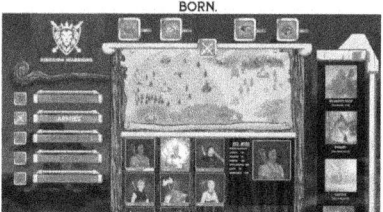

WILL YOU JOIN US FOR THE FIGHT OF YOUR LIFE?

THIS KINGDOM GOD IDEA IN 70 DAYS GREW TO OVER 60 COUNTRIES AND 24 LANGUAGES SEEING TRANSFORMATIONS OF IDENTITY!

WE HAVE AMAZING ARTIST & DEVELOPER WHO HAVE WORKED WITH SONY, DISNEY, & MARVEL

JOIN HERE!

KINGDOMWARRIORSNFT.COM

  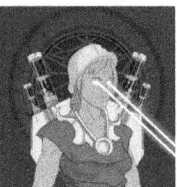

www.ingramcontent.com/pod-product-compliance
Lightning Source LLC
Chambersburg PA
CBHW071409210526
45465CB00001B/312